WHAT OTHERS

"David Curry's life and personal story are an example of how God can use a man of integrity who is committed to and persistent to serving Him. His personal story will be a blessing to you."
— Zig Ziglar, *author and motivational speaker*

"I am blessed to be a part of David Curry's life story. It has been rewarding to see how the Lord has broken Dave over the years. His life story will leave an imprint on your heart and be a blessing to you as well."
— Bill McCartney, *founder of Promise Keepers*

"Some people educate, some motivate, some entertain. Only a few like David Curry do it all. His integrity and wisdom speak louder than words. Everyone is richer for having listened to and thought with David Curry."
— Charlie "Tremendous" Jones, *author and speaker*

"I have known David Curry for a number of years. He was the first recipient of our Kingdom Builder award for our school in New York City in 1995. His life story will be a Kingdom Builder experience for you."
— Tom Maharis, *president, City Vision and Transformation Life Center*

Mini-Messages
FOR
Monday through Friday

Biblical–Inspirational–Motivational
DAILY MESSAGES

Blessings To You

David W. Curry

David Curry's Mini-Messages for Monday through Friday

Published by
Executive Books
206 West Allen Street
Mechanicsburg, PA 17055
www.ExecutiveBooks.com

Copyright © 2005 by David W. Curry

All rights reserved. No part of this book may be reproduced or transmitted in any form or by any means, electronic or mechanical, including photocopying, recording, or by any information storage and retrieval system, without the written permission of the publisher, except where permitted by law.

Book Design by Boulder Bookworks, Boulder, CO

ISBN: 1-933715-03-0

Printed in the United States of America

Originally published by Diamond Publishing, Morrison, CO

DEDICATION

To Amy

*My wonderful wife of forty-four years,
who has always been my biggest cheerleader
for everything I do, including this book.
Thanks so much for your unconditional love,
your dedication, and commitment
to make life wonderful.*

—D.C.

Contents

Acknowledgements ix

Foreword by Bill McCartney................................. xi

Introduction.. xiii

On a Personal Note From My Heart to Yours.................. xv

Mini-Messages for Monday through Friday 1

Ordering Information 261

Acknowledgements

I didn't realize how much was involved in writing a book until I wrote this one. It takes a lot of people doing so many different things to complete the project.

I would like to thank my wonderful wife, not only for her love and dedication to me, but for the countless hours she spent talking to people, going back and forth to the printers dozens of times, for reviewing my materials, and for ideas and suggestions on how to make the book better. Her wisdom was very helpful in completing this project. I would especially like to acknowledge my wonderful administrative assistant Desireé Dillon. Even though I live in Denver and she lives in the Bay area of California, she made this project run so very smoothly. All the pages were first handwritten, but she performed miracles in taking that bad handwriting and transcribing it on the computer with very few corrections. She went the extra mile by working nights and weekends to help complete the project on time. Words can never describe how much I appreciate all her hard work.

I would also like to thank the wonderful people at Day of Discovery who publish the *Daily Bread*. I have read the devotional for thirty-four years, and many of the ideas and messages here come from reading the Bible along with their devotional.

In addition, I want to acknowledge Alan Bernhard and Alan Stark of Boulder Bookworks for doing the impossible and putting forth the extra commitment necessary to meet the deadlines I needed for completion.

Last but not least, I want to thank my Heavenly Father for not only loving me enough to send his Son to die for me, but also for the leading by the Holy Spirit to put onto paper what He spoke to my heart each day. He is the real author and finisher of this project.

Foreword

by

BILL MCCARTNEY

My eleventh year as the head football coach at the University of Colorado was 1992. That summer, Promise Keepers hosted its first stadium event at Folsom Field in Boulder. That fall, I met David Curry, a man whom I would come to love and admire as one of God's special gifts to me. He called my office, made an appointment, and arranged to meet and discuss difficult issues over a period of several months. I can vividly recall how wholeheartedly Dave dealt with spiritual matters. He demonstrated a tender and broken heart, and I was drawn to this humble, talented guy. These intense private conversations were bathed in prayer and served to help him come to terms with the birth of his biracial grandson Braxton.

He now shares that experience in his life story all over the country, and I feel privileged to have been a part of that story. It has been rewarding the past twelve years to see how the Lord has challenged Dave and used him for His glory. As a professional speaker, Dave has a unique way of reaching into the hearts of people. He has a passion for souls and wants to see people come to Christ, and not only live an abundant life here on earth, but a glorious life with our Savior in heaven.

For some time, Dave has prayed for God to give him an effective tool to not only reach people for Christ, but also give them the opportunity to get into the Bible and learn the milk of the word as new babes in Christ. In his personal time with the Lord, Dave started using a system that helped him to remember not only what God said to him day-to-day, but also how he could apply it. One year into the process, God spoke to Dave and told him to put it into a book as the tools he had been praying for. As a result, *Mini-Messages for Monday through Friday* was born.

This book resulted from Dave's personal time with the Lord. I think it is one of the most unique devotional books I have read for reaching people for Christ and then getting them immediately into the Word with scriptures, a short daily message, and an application they can apply every day for the first year as a new believer. This book is written the same way that Dave speaks, which is simple, practical, and to the point.

Dave also cares about mending the broken hearts of others through the love of Christ; the same love that mended his broken heart. This book will also help to do just that. As you read this book, ask God to show you how to apply these simple principles for your own personal growth, but also how you can share the same message with others. I know you will be blessed for doing so.

— *Bill McCartney*

Introduction

For the past thirty-four years, I have started my day with the Lord in prayer and Bible reading. One of the other key pieces of literature that has been a blessing to me is the *Daily Bread* from Radio Bible Class. I have hardly missed a day in these thirty-four years of reading their daily devotional during my quiet time.

One of my weaknesses, however, is that during the day, I get so busy that I forget what I read at 6:00 A.M. I have talked to a number of people who have the same problem. Some of the ways I remember and learn best is through quotes, acronyms, and stories. When I worked for my good friend Zig Ziglar for eight years, I always remembered his stories, as they made it much easier for me to remember the principle behind the story. Another way I remember and learn well is through three-point outlines, each beginning with the same letter. As a result, I began a new method of using my Bible and the *Daily Bread* devotional. As I read the scriptures and the devotional, I looked for a common theme or thread, and any words that jumped out at me and started with the same letter.

As I began this process, I recorded it in my daily journal. I would find these three key words and then write what it was saying to my heart. I did this for 18 months, and one morning, God spoke to my heart and said that I should put them into book form. My wife has a prayer ministry that she calls Mini-Miracles, where she prays and records answers to prayer requests that are small miracles to some people, but are important to her. Over the years, she has seen scores of answers through her Mini-Miracle prayers. As a result, God spoke to my heart and told me to title my devotional book *Mini-Messages for Monday through Friday: Biblical—Inspirational—Motivational Daily Messages.*

The scriptures are those recommended by Radio Bible Class, and my mini-messages come from those three key words or phrases in each message that begin with the same letter. I encourage you to do what I do each day. After reading your message, write those three words on a 3" x 5" card, and throughout the day, just glance at that card and immediately you will recall what you read earlier in the day, so God can continue to speak to you. It has really worked for me, and it is my prayer that it will work for you as well. May God bless your heart and spirit as you read *Mini-Messages for Monday through Friday.*

ON A PERSONAL NOTE
FROM MY HEART TO YOURS

Three Key Words:
Message — Ministry — Mission

I. MESSAGE

In your journey through this book you will have 260 messages which represent five messages per week for 52 weeks. These are personal messages that God gave to my heart in my daily quiet time with Him. I have tried to make them simple and to the point, but also with a message that will encourage and help you as you start or end your day.

II. MINISTRY

An additional objective in writing this book was to have the messages minister to you personally. I recently read a statement that said millions of people go to bed each night starving for food, but tens of millions go to bed each night starving for some type of recognition or acceptance. That spoke to my heart; that we have millions of hurting people in this world. Therefore, I asked the Lord to help me write my messages with the hope and prayer that they minister to some hurting hearts. Jesus ministered to hurting people while He was on earth and I hope He will do the same for you as you use this book.

III. MISSION

The real purpose behind this book comes from my personal mission in life. Like many of you, I have a number of family members and close friends who don't know Christ as their personal Lord and Savior. It really breaks my heart. For those of you who know the Lord as your Savior, this book will bless you, but for those who don't, you will not get the full blessing from this book until you receive the Lord. Therefore, God has told me that I should give everyone who does not know the Lord as Savior the opportunity to do so before they read the first chapter. As a result, I am going to share with you why this is a personal mission for me by using what God says in His Word, the Bible. One thing the Bible is very clear on is truth, as it says you shall know the truth and the truth shall set you free. I believe the Bible is truth.

In my life story, "Fear—Failure—Frustration and Freedom," I always close with the following truth from the word, so I am going to share it with you just like I present it to an audience. The Bible says that God created everything, including a place called heaven, a place called earth, and a place called hell. You don't hear much about hell today, but it is a real place. It also says that when we die, we are going to spend eternity in either heaven or hell. In other words, there are no other options. It also states that heaven is a place of beauty, peace, joy and total contentment. No *sickness*, no *sorrows*, no *suffering*. However, hell is a place of torment with nothing but *sickness*, *sorrow* and unbearable *suffering*. Jesus said that He did not come into the world to condemn it, but through Him the world might be saved. In other words, God doesn't want anybody to go to hell and does not send us to hell, but gave us the choice. We choose where to spend eternity, so here is an important question to ask yourself: "If I should die today, or when I die, am I absolutely sure I will spend eternity in heaven?" If at this moment you cannot answer "yes" to that question, then you can settle that issue before you read the first chapter of this book.

I am going to give you the truth from the Bible on how to receive the Savior right where you are and make a reservation for heaven. I am asking God to speak to your heart as I write this truth.

The Bible says, "All have sinned and come short of the glory of God." Therefore, we are all sinners. It also tells us that the wages of sin is death. Since Adam and Eve committed sin in the garden, there has been death. The Bible also says, "It is appointed unto man once to die and then the judgment." So we are born, we sin, we die, and we are judged for our sins. As I said previously, the wages of sin is death, but the gift of God is eternal life through Jesus Christ our Lord. In other words, forgiveness of sin is a gift of God. We cannot earn or buy it. Why? The Bible says, "For by grace you are saved through faith and that not of yourselves, it is a gift of God, not of works lest any man should boast." God is saying that if we could buy it or earn it through being good, going to church, singing in the choir, or putting money in the offering plate, we would brag or boast about how good we are. Again, it is a gift. So how do you receive this gift? The Bible says, "If thou shall confess with thy mouth, the Lord Jesus and believe in thine heart that God hath raised Him from the dead thou shall be saved, for with the heart man believeth unto righteousness and with the mouth confession is made unto salvation."

If we believe that Jesus is the Son of God, died on the cross for our sins and arose the third day, and ask Him to forgive us and come into our heart and be our Lord and Savior, we now know Him and when we die, we will go to heaven. You don't have to hope anymore because the truth from the Bible says, "These things I write that ye may know—not hope—but know that you have eternal life."

After reading these pages, if you would like to receive Christ into your heart, not only to go to heaven when you die, but also to have a more fulfilled life while here on this earth, I would invite you to pray this short prayer:

Dear Jesus, I believe that you are the Son of God, that you died on the cross for my sins, that you arose again, and dear Jesus, I ask you to forgive me of my sins and come into my heart and be my Lord and Savior. Help me to live for you this day forward. In your name, Amen.

If you prayed that prayer, you can now rest assured that your next home will be in heaven forever. Also, if you did so, you helped me in carrying out my mission. I am so happy for you and I want to welcome you into the family of God.

Now that you have done so, and you begin your journey in your faith, these messages will help you grow daily and hopefully be a blessing to you.

Never forget—Jesus loves you and so do I.

In Christ,

Your brother,

David Curry

WEEK 1—MONDAY

Christ the Servant

SCRIPTURE READING: John 13:1–17
THREE KEY WORDS: Humble—Hands—Heart

I. Humble

In today's scripture, we see how important it is to be humble. We see Jesus saying, "I came to serve and not to be served." Today many people think they are better than anyone else. The corporate president, the entertainer, and the professional athlete all want to be served. The greatest person and most powerful person to walk the earth and help create the earth said, "Be an example. Humble yourselves and serve."

II. Hands

Today we see the hands that shaped the universe and created all things. We see the King of Kings and Lord of Lords taking these hands and doing a lowly job of washing feet. When I pictured this, I envisioned the shoeshine man and the important task he does, but also a picture of what Jesus was doing. However, the shoeshine man cleans only dirty shoes, but the Master was cleaning dirty feet! What a servant.

III. Heart

The example Jesus gives us today tells us that we are to surrender our heart and let Him use our hands and feet to tell others about Him. These hands that washed the feet are the same hands that were nailed to the cross for our dirty heart. Therefore, by accepting Him, we not only have clean feet, but a pure heart. Oh, what a savior. Oh, what a servant. Go forth and do likewise.

APPLICATION: As we pray, ask Jesus to give us a humble heart. Tell Him you want to be more like Him. When you see someone today who is less fortunate than you, have a servant's heart and help them out. If Jesus can wash feet, we can do whatever it takes to serve like Him today.

WEEK 1—TUESDAY

Strife

SCRIPTURE READING: Proverbs 26:17–21
THREE KEY WORDS: Conflict—Consequences—Compassion

I. Conflict

Strife brings conflict. Conflict brings confrontation, and confrontation brings casualties. Unfortunately, a great deal of this takes place in the body of Christ. We let strife take place over surrender, and our flesh gets in the way. Before long, all of the above happens. The Bible says that words or deeds spoken in anger or bitterness are of the devil and cause a lot of hurt.

II. Consequences

The consequences of conflict are sometimes so hurtful that they can last a lifetime. I know a Christian couple who, from the beginning of their marriage, have been in constant conflict, and the consequences have been so hurtful that their relationships with their children and siblings have been damaged forever. What a price to pay because of the flesh.

III. Compassion

When strife enters our lives, remember the compassion Christ had for people in His life. Whenever He was confronted with stress or strife, in most cases He showed compassion and so should we. Ask yourself the famous question, "What would Jesus do?"

APPLICATION: If someone is causing *conflict* in your life, go to them in *compassion* and get it settled to avoid the *consequences*.

WEEK 1—WEDNESDAY

When in Trouble—Pray

SCRIPTURE READING: 2 Kings 19:1–19
THREE KEY WORDS: Harm—Hopeless—Honor

I. Harm

When we face harm and everything seems hopeless, we need to cry out to God for help. There is no situation or problem too big or too small that God won't hear when we talk to Him. Also, there is nothing too big or too small that God can't handle if we will let Him. We need to open our hearts and have a talk with God and just simply say, "What shall I do? Please help me."

II. Hopeless

The Savior is there when we lose hope. Hope is sometimes the only thing we have left. There is an old saying that there are no hopeless situations in life. We simply lose hope in certain situations. God the Father is always there to help us.

III. Honor

No matter how hopeless it may seem or what harm we face, to get help from God the Father, we should honor Him at all times by letting Him be first in our life and stand for what is right. We ask our children to honor us. We should honor our heavenly Father as children of God as well.

APPLICATION: No matter what is going on in your life right now that is causing you harm or making you feel hopeless, open your Bible and have a little talk with God. Honor and praise Him, and sit still and let God work.

WEEK 1—THURSDAY

Going Home

SCRIPTURE READING: Luke 24:36–53
THREE KEY WORDS: Worship—Witness—Word

I. Worship
As Jesus was getting ready to go home to be with the Father, He told the disciples that He would send another Comforter—the Holy Spirit. Then He instructed them with things they could do with that power. One of the things God desires most from us is powerful worship. Jesus said the Holy Spirit's power in worship will make His presence real to us, so much so that we will continually want to praise and worship Him for what He has done for us.

II. Witness
Jesus also said we would have the power of the Holy Spirit to witness for Him. In fact, He commanded us to go into the world with His gospel. We cannot do it effectively in the flesh, so if we are to be effective witnesses, we are to get energized by tapping into the power of the Holy Spirit.

III. Word
Jesus also said we must study the Word of God so our minds and eyes are opened like the disciples' were when He quoted scripture to them. We must have God's Word stored in our heart for *powerful worship*, *powerful witness*, and *powerful prayer*. Lord, please help me.

APPLICATION: Study God's Word and ask Him to fill you with His power. Give praise and worship to Him for doing so. Then get out and be a witness today.

WEEK 1—FRIDAY

This Little Light of Mine

SCRIPTURE READING: John 1:1–14
THREE KEY WORDS: Light—Love—Life

I. Light
There is a little song that says, "This little light of mine, I'm going to let it shine." In today's scripture reading, God is talking about us being a light to the world. People are walking around in the dark, not even knowing what is happening. Have you ever stood in a totally dark room all by yourself, with no light around anywhere? If you waited ten seconds, you might have started to feel lost and frightened. Then, suddenly you might just see a crack of light and your fear is gone. That is the way of the world. They might not know it, but they are in total darkness and are on their way to outer darkness in hell. It is our job as Christians to be that crack of light in the door, to not only give them hope but to take the bright Light of Christ to this dark and frightened world.

II. Love
"God loved us so much that He gave His only begotten Son that whosoever believed in Him should not perish, but have everlasting life." That is the Light of the World. John came to bear witness of that Light that all, through Him, might be saved. When Christ came into the world, many did not receive Him, but those who did became His children. We should love Him because He first loved us. The Bible tells us that if you truly love someone, you will lay down your life for that person, and that is what Christ did for us. We must show that same love by laying aside our busy schedules, our work, our hobbies; and go talk to someone about this wonderful Light. That is real love.

III. Life
When we take the Love of Light to those of the lost world, that will not only give them eternal life, but they also become a light for Christ. That is real life for the believer. If you want a real purpose in life and you want to be *energized*, *excited*, and *enthusiastic*, then be an *example* by taking the light of Christ to a friend, relative, neighbor, or someone at work. You will find real life in doing so.

APPLICATION: Today, take time to thank God for bringing His Light to you. Then earnestly seek Him and ask Him to bring someone to you today or point you to someone you should go see to share this wonderful Light.

WEEK 2—MONDAY
The Holy Spirit

SCRIPTURE READING: Galatians 5:15–26
THREE KEY WORDS: Presence—Power—Person

I. Presence
When we ask Christ to come into our lives, He gives us the presence of the Holy Spirit. The Holy Spirit lives in our body, His temple. We need to take time to build a relationship with Him. He is present with us everywhere we go, including the places we should not go. He wants us to be His best friends, to help us, and comfort us.

II. Power
Just like it is difficult to explain the power of electricity and how it comes on when we flip a switch, it is also hard to explain the power of the Holy Spirit. The power is there, like a battery in a car, but we can only tap into that power by releasing our total being to Him to guide and direct us. When we tap into that power, we can accomplish so much more and feel energized instead of feeling empty.

III. Person
The Holy Spirit is the third Person of the Trinity. He is just as much a person as Jesus was while He was here on earth. He loves us more than anyone else and wants to spend time with us so we can build a loving, living, and long-lasting, relationship with Him. There is nothing like being in the constant presence of the Holy Spirit.

APPLICATION: Take time today to just have a genuine conversation with the Holy Spirit. Tell Him how much you love Him. Ask Him to fill you so much that His presence will overwhelm you.

WEEK 2—TUESDAY

Is Life Really Good?

SCRIPTURE READING: Psalm 34
THREE KEY WORDS: Good—Gifted—Godly

I. Good
God has some requirements that determine if life is good, bad, or, ugly. Some of those requirements are spelled out in today's scripture. They are not always easy, but nothing in life that is good is ever easy. First He says to watch your tongue about lying. Also, turn from all known sins. Spend your time doing good. Live in peace with everyone. If we do this, God will hear our prayers and help us out of our troubles. He will pardon us and provide for us. Wow!

II. Gifted
God has given us gifts that we should use for Him and others. When we use our gifts for others, this will add to our good life because we can encourage others and make their lives a little better as well. The gift of love and encouragement for God and neighbor is the greatest gift of all.

III. Godly
To receive the benefits of the good life and gifted life, we must live a godly life. It says in verse 15 that He is watching us and gives attention when we cry to Him, but in verse 16, it says the Lord has made up His mind to wipe out the memory of ungodly men. How sad. We are to be Holy because He is Holy. That is truly the "good life."

APPLICATION: Let's do our best to be good, godly, and holy. Think of someone you know right now who needs the gift of love and encouragement. Pray for them and then write them a note or give them a call. Your life will be better because you did.

WEEK 2—WEDNESDAY

God's Little Child

SCRIPTURE READING: Psalm 103
THREE KEY WORDS: Unworthy —Understanding —Unconditional

I. **Unworthy**
Sometimes Satan will tell us we are unworthy, that we don't deserve anything, and that we can never be good enough for anyone, especially not good enough for God. This will cause us to think we are unwanted by others or by God, but Satan is a liar.

II. **Understanding**
God understands how Satan makes us feel. Every physical, mental, and psychological problem we have faced, Jesus faced on the cross. He knows every pain, every hurt, and every need. The Bible says that His understanding is unlimited.

III. **Unconditional**
Although we feel unwanted and unworthy, God loves us unconditionally. The Bible says that we are God's spiritual masterpiece—a flawless jewel in God's eyes. That makes us valuable. There are several examples in the Bible. "He forgives all my sins as far as the east is from the west. He ransomed me from hell. He showers me with loving kindness and tender mercies. He never bears a grudge." He is my Father and loves me no matter what. That makes me God's special child.

APPLICATION: Find someone you know today who is feeling unworthy and unwanted and show them the same love God has for you. Make that person feel special.

WEEK 2—THURSDAY

Everything Has Its Consequences

SCRIPTURE READING: Exodus 20:1–17
THREE KEY WORDS: Inheritance—Influence—Integrity

I. Inheritance
God says in Proverbs that our children and grandchildren are our greatest inheritance. He also says that we are to be an example to them. We are to lead by example so they will follow. The greatest inheritance we can leave our family is a godly memory of us.

II. Influence
God says in Exodus 20:5–6 that if He punishes us because we are sinning, that the punishment and influence will continue upon our children and grandchildren. The Bible is full of examples. That is why we must be a godly influence. If I walk away from God, my children might walk away with me. If my influence is godly and I walk with Him daily, my family may follow.

III. Integrity
This whole example comes down to being a godly person of integrity. Integrity is the most important foundation stone of our Christian walk and Christian example to our children, grandchildren, and great-grandchildren. I once heard someone ask a famous speaker, "What is your definition of integrity and character?" I will never forget his simple answer; "What you do when nobody is looking, or what you do in the dark." Great answer!

APPLICATION: Every time you are tempted to do wrong, remember your inheritance and your influence, and then do the right thing to keep your integrity intact. It will be worth it.

WEEK 2 — FRIDAY

This Love Is So Compelling

SCRIPTURE READING: II Corinthians 5:9–15
THREE KEY PHRASES: Compelling Love of Christ—Compelling Love for Christ—Compelling Love Through Christ

I. Compelling Love of Christ
Christ loved us so much that He voluntarily laid down His life and suffered pain, shame, agony, and put all of our sins on His shoulders. He did this so we could be reconciled to God the Father, saved from hell, and able to spend eternity with Him in heaven. That compelling love should persuade us to live for Him at all times.

II. Compelling Love for Christ
Because of what Christ did for us on the cross, we should be compelled every day not to do anything that would hurt or grieve Him or make Him sad. The wrath of God should not motivate us to do right. Our compelling love for Him and what He did should motivate us to live for Him daily. We should not live to please ourselves or man, but to please our heavenly Father and Brother.

III. Compelling Love through Christ
We should take this life-changing love to others and show them and tell them of this compelling love of Christ so they can be reconciled to God and have a compelling love for Christ. Most of all, because we have such compelling love for others, we want to save them from hell. We have a great commission to do so.

APPLICATION: Take time today to thank God for His compelling love for us and then ask Him to show you someone who He can love through you. Next, pray and ask Him to give you the desire, strength, and love to do so.

WEEK 3—MONDAY

Tough Love

SCRIPTURE READING: Hebrews 12:1–11
THREE KEY WORDS: Correction—Chastening—Caring

I. Correction

Whenever we get off base or out of line in our relationship with God, He has to correct us. When a ship at sea gets off its course, the captain must do what he has to do to avoid a possible crash. God has to do the same with us. He doesn't want us to crash and burn, so He corrects us so we can get back in line to walk with Him. It is always good for us.

II. Chastening

When we go too far and we continually disobey God, He has to chastise us. Just like an earthly father has to chastise his child who disobeys, our heavenly Father must do the same. In fact, the Bible says that those God loves, He chastens. Therefore, if you feel like God is chastening you for some reason, it should make you feel good. It proves your salvation and that you are one of His precious children. Being chastised doesn't always make us feel joyful, and it is often painful. But it is always done with love, because it is good for us.

III. Caring

God corrects us and chastises us because He cares so much for us. He loves us so much that He must do so. As parents, we do the same because we care so much for our children. God cares so much more that He sent His only child to die for us. That is truly a caring Father.

APPLICATION: If you are off course today and you feel God is correcting or chastising you, then first of all, thank Him for being your caring Father. Then ask His forgiveness and get back in line. You will be glad you did, and He will be very happy.

WEEK 3—TUESDAY

The Glory of God

SCRIPTURE READING: Ezekiel 43:1–5
THREE KEY WORDS: Goodness—Greatness—Glory

I. Goodness

God is so good to us even during our tough times. He promises that He will never leave or forsake us. He will supply all of our needs, but not our wants. No matter what we do, whether in the past, present, or future, all our sins are forgiven and forgotten. What a good God we have. Therefore, we need to be good to our Father in return.

II. Greatness

There are no problems too big or too small for our great and good God. He is so great that He can remove any mountain in our life. In His greatness, He created everything, including us, and He doesn't make any mistakes. "Great is His faithfulness and His mercy endureth forever."

III. Glory

Just as God showed His glory in verse 43, and also to Moses in the Old Testament, someday when Christ returns, we will see the greatest glory of all. That will be when we see the face of Jesus. Like the old song says, "It will be worth it all when we see Jesus; it will be worth it all when we see Christ. One look at His sweet face all sorrow will erase. So quickly run the race, 'til we see Christ. Oh, what glory it will be when our Jesus we will see. Glory to God."

APPLICATION: Thank God today for His goodness and greatness in your life. As you start your day, live it as if Christ were coming today, because He just might do so.

WEEK 3—WEDNESDAY

God's Word

SCRIPTURE READING: 2 Timothy 2:14–16
THREE KEY WORDS: Study—Standards—Strength

I. Study
We are students of God's Word, therefore, we should study God's Word. The Word of God is what changes our hearts and minds. We also need to know the truth from God's Word so we can keep our faith strong. A solid foundation comes from studying God's Word.

II. Standards
God's Word has standards we should live by. All the standards for living the Christian life are in God's Word. In this passage, Paul says not to argue over foolish questions. He talks about how to treat others, run from temptation to avoid sin, be humble when you teach others, and about family and business standards. All of these life problems are addressed in God's Word.

III. Strength
If we study God's Word, we will also gain strength when we need it most. In verses 11 and 12, Paul says that even when we are too weak to have any faith left, God still remains faithful to us and will help us. He cannot disown us since we are a part of Him. The Word also says that He will always carry out His promises. When we are weak, we are made strong through God's grace and God's Word.

APPLICATION: If you have questions about some standards in your life or you are weak in your faith right now, look to God's Word. Then pray for strength and ask Him to give you some specific answers. Set aside just a few minutes a day to study God's Word. If you have a concordance in your Bible, look up the specific subject that is bothering you and study all of the recommended verses.

WEEK 3—THURSDAY

I Was Blind But Now I See

SCRIPTURE READING: Colossians 1:1–18

THREE KEY WORDS: The Sight of Salvation—The Scariness of Salvation—The Security of Salvation

I. The Sight of Salvation

Apostle Paul was blinded so he could see Christ and salvation. We were just like Paul. We were blind to the gospel and salvation. We did not see the simple plan God had for us. We had to try and figure it out. Then, like Paul, one day the scales were removed from our eyes, and we saw Christ and His plan of salvation.

II. The Scariness of Salvation

Just like a person who receives physical sight for the first time can be somewhat frightened by the unknown things they see, we are sometimes frightened or feel scared about our new life in Christ. What will our friends and family think or say? How should I tell them? How should I act? What now? What next?

III. The Security of Salvation

We have the security that God is always with us here on earth after our salvation experience and also the security of going to heaven when we die. As Paul said, there is no other way to heaven. God chose us to be a part of His family forever, and that should bring us real security.

APPLICATION: If you are a fairly new Christian and you are somewhat fearful of what to do, find another person, either a family member, friend, co-worker, or classmate, to help. Also, as you start your new walk with Christ, start reading your Bible daily. I suggest you start in the book of John; then Matthew, Mark, and Luke. Also, read one chapter from Proverbs each day. There are thirty-one chapters in Proverbs, one for each day of the month. It is full of wisdom on how to live your new-found life.

WEEK 3—FRIDAY

How Do You Measure Love?

SCRIPTURE READING: 1 John 4:1–21
THREE KEY WORDS: Measure—Mercy—Ministry

I. Measure
We can see how much we love Jesus by the way we love others. If we don't show real love to the unloved, then we cannot love Jesus as we should. We deserve to be unloved by Jesus, but He loves us so much that He laid down His life for us. That is real love. The Bible says that real love should cause us to lay down our lives for others.

II. Mercy
We are not to be harsh and judgmental of others, but like God had mercy on us, we are to have mercy on others. We can show our measure of love by having mercy on someone who has wronged us or hurt us by forgiving them like God had mercy on us and forgave us. Mercy and grace are two of the things we as Christians find hard to understand, and the only way we can truly experience them is to be a living example of mercy and grace.

III. Ministry
Our ministry of love is to show a great measure of mercy and love by telling them about the love of Jesus and sharing the gospel with them. Then, they can experience for themselves this great love that God has for us by sending His one and only Son to die for us. Oh, what a measure of love this is. Oh, what mercy we have received.

APPLICATION: Think of someone you know who may have hurt or wronged you in some way. Then meditate on how we wronged or hurt Christ before we received His mercy. Next, go and tell them how much you love them and forgive them and tell them why. This will be a living example of the gospel of Christ doing the same for them.

WEEK 4—MONDAY

Godly Character

SCRIPTURE READING: Romans 12:1–5
THREE KEY PHRASES: Shape Us—Show Us—Save Us

I. Shape Us
God says we are to let Him shape us by transforming our minds and hearts through His Word. We should not allow the behaviors and philosophies of the world to shape our lives and characteristics. We need to let God's Word shape us to be holy and acceptable unto Him.

II. Show Us
God will be our source and show us through His Spirit how to be godly people. He tells us to be honest with ourselves, measuring our value by how much faith God has given us. God has given each of us the ability to serve Him, and we are to use it to serve and show others about Christ.

III. Save Us
God will save us from the shaping of the world if we allow Him to shape us through the power of the Holy Spirit. To be a living sacrifice for God, holy and acceptable unto Him, we are to walk in the fruit of the Spirit and let the Spirit be our source.

APPLICATION: The way we shape ourselves to be godly is by the transforming and renewing of our minds. Therefore, as you study God's scripture today, ask Him to show you His will with the same power that saved you, because it can also shape you. Keep the Word fresh in your mind all day long.

WEEK 4—TUESDAY

Be Kind in Criticism

SCRIPTURE READING: Galatians 6:1–5
THREE KEY WORDS: Gentle—Gracious—Grace

I. Gentle
When we see a brother fall in sin, we are not to kick him while he is down. The Bible says to restore him with gentleness and meekness. We must not compromise our standards to do so, but we need to help him get back. Christ is gentle with love and chastisement, and we need to be as well.

II. Gracious
Christians have been accused for a long time of killing their wounded by their words or actions. Words can build or destroy. When we have hard feelings against a brother, we should be gracious and not gruff. The best way to criticize is through the direction of the Holy Spirit with gentleness and graciousness.

III. Grace
When God sees we need to be chastised, He does not beat us up, but restores us by His grace through gentleness and graciousness. If Jesus can show that kind of love for us, then we should show that kind of love for others. God is love, and we should be also.

APPLICATION: Ask God to show you someone you know who has been treated so badly by his brothers and sisters in Christ that he is really suffering and needs someone to talk to. He might be so bitter that he has even left the church. Go to those brothers or sisters and pray with them and try to restore them in gentleness and graciousness, as this is what Jesus would do.

WEEK 4—WEDNESDAY

Fatherly Love for Children

SCRIPTURE READING: Hosea 11
THREE KEY WORDS: Raising Children—Rebellious Children—
  Returning Children

I. Raising Children
One of the hardest jobs a parent has is raising godly children. Just like God with Israel, we train them to walk and talk. We hold them in our arms, we feed them, and we have good times together. It is a rough responsibility today to raise godly children, and we cannot do it without God's help.

II. Rebellious Children
Even though we give it our best, sometimes things don't turn out as we liked or hoped. Our children will rebel. Just like Israel rebelled against God, our children will sometimes rebel against us. We then go through great sorrow and pain. We want to *punish*, but we must try *prayer* instead. We see their tragic mistakes and ask ourselves, "How can they forget? How could they do this? Where did I go wrong?" But Romans 8:28 says that all things will work out for good.

III. Returning Children
God promised us in His Word that our children will return. Just like Israel came back to Him and just like the prodigal son came home, so will our children. It may take a long time, and result in a lot of hurt, but we have the promise from God that they will return. He says to train up a child in the way they should go and when they are older they will return.

APPLICATION: If you are raising young children, it will be one of the hardest things you do for the next few years. Take time for your children; not just quality time, but quantity time, and teach them to be godly. If your children are away from you and in rebellion, just remember to pray for them daily, show them unconditional love, and ask God to bring them back. He will guide you and comfort you in this difficult time.

WEEK 4—THURSDAY

What to Do with Wealth

SCRIPTURE READING: Luke 12:13–21
THREE KEY WORDS: Worry—Work—Wealth

I. Worry

When it comes to our future, sometimes we worry. We can get frustrated because we don't see a way to slow down. Jesus said, "My Father knows every need I have, and He will always give me my needs if I put the kingdom first." He didn't say He would meet our wants, but He did say He would meet our needs. Don't always be wishing for what you don't have. Real life and real living are not related to how wealthy we are.

II. Work

In order to get where we need to be for our future, we sometime have to continue to work. There is no other way. We can kill ourselves working to get wealth, but in the end, as Solomon says, it is all futile. We all die. The thing we need to do is be thankful that we have the health to work and a good job or a business. We have to either find something else we enjoy more in our work, or we can just take it one day at a time.

III. Wealth

Jesus said that our real wealth and treasure is not here, but in heaven. Our Father has many mansions. One of those is for me, and one of those is for you. The work I do for Him down here will build my wealth in heaven, and it will be greater than any wealth we can have while here on earth. That's a promise from our heavenly Father.

APPLICATION: As we strive each day to work hard, make ends meet, and save for our future, remember what the Lord said in the book of Matthew: "Where our treasure is, that's where our heart will be also." Someday, when we get to heaven, it will be worth every hard day's work on earth to invest in His Kingdom. There's no greater return on our investment than in the Kingdom of God.

WEEK 4—FRIDAY

How Do We Handle Daily Pain?

SCRIPTURE READING: 2 Corinthians 5:1–10
THREE KEY WORDS: Painful Bodies—Perishing Bodies—Perfect Bodies

I. Painful Bodies
We all suffer pain in our bodies. The older we get, the more pain we seem to have. That is just the way it is. So many people who have *pain* on the outside have *peace* on the inside because of the *promise* of Christ—that He is with us all the time and this pain will some day be over. We need this peace of mind.

II. Perishing Bodies
The fact is that our bodies are decaying and someday our bodies will all perish. Paul said that we are just a tent here and someday that tent will be let down, but when that happens, we will receive new permanent bodies when we die and go to heaven.

III. Perfect Bodies
Paul said that when we die and go to heaven we won't be only a spirit, but we will slip into a permanent body. This body will be perfect. Paul says in verse 1 that our new bodies will be perfect, made by God, with no pain, aches, sickness, emotional hurt, but perfect, permanent bodies with our spirit, living eternally with Jesus our Lord and Savior forever.

APPLICATION: As you face a day of pain and sickness, which sometimes seems unbearable, go to the Word of God and ask Him to give you scripture to comfort you. Remember how He healed the sick, and also remember that someday, when you get to heaven, you will have a perfect permanent body with no more pain. That is the focus we must have daily to make it through another day.

WEEK 5—MONDAY

The Importance of Heaven

SCRIPTURE READING: Mark 10:11–22
THREE KEY WORDS: Earthly—Eternal—Entering

I. **Earthly**
Like the rich young ruler in verse 10, we sometimes let earthly possessions get in the way of heaven, or for that matter, living for Christ. The people of the world focus on the importance of living for good times and great things here on earth, and don't make heaven their priority. Compared to here, heaven will be absolutely unbelievable.

II. **Eternal**
Jesus once said, "Where your heart is, there your treasure will be also." A lot of important rich people here on earth will have little in heaven. Many poor and humble people here will be rich and great in heaven because their *priority* was *purpose* for Christ and not worldly *possessions*.

III. **Entering**
Jesus said that it is almost impossible for a rich person to enter heaven, but when we enter heaven it will be full of riches; streets of gold, walls of jasper, diamonds, jewels, but most of all, we will have the richest life possible by spending eternity with Christ and our loved ones.

APPLICATION: As we go out each day and face the pressures of trying to be accepted or promoted in the workplace so that we may gain more riches, we must remember that we are only passing through here on earth; our permanent home is in heaven. We should never let our fleshly desires keep us from enjoying the spiritual life and eternity of heaven.

WEEK 5—TUESDAY

Criticism or Compliments

SCRIPTURE READING: 2 Samuel 1:17–27
THREE KEY WORDS: Faults—Failures—Favor

I. Faults

Everyone we meet in life has faults and flaws. Certainly David did with Bathsheba and also with Saul, who hated him and tried to kill him. David chose to focus on Saul's good qualities and not his faults. As Christians, we are to find the good in others as well, because when we can *focus* on their *fruits* and not their *faults*, we can become their friends.

II. Failures

Everyone we meet has failed in some area of his or her life, but as Zig Ziglar says, "Failure is an event, not a person." David had a great failure in his life, and yet he found favor with God, and God used him greatly. God can greatly use our failures as well if we will let Him.

III. Favor

If we are Christ-like, we not only find fault and failures in people, but we can also find favor. In other words, there is something good in everyone. If we focus on the good and encourage people, we can help them turn their *faults* and *failures* into *fruit*, so look for the good in others.

APPLICATION: Today, as you go out into the world and rub shoulders with people at work or play, find the good in others. Give someone a sincere compliment. It will make that person's day better, as well as yours.

WEEK 5—WEDNESDAY

The Certainty of Death

SCRIPTURE READING: 2 Timothy 4:6–18
THREE KEY PHRASES: Death Is Planned—Death Is Peaceful—
Death Is Purposeful

I. Death is Planned
Because of the sin in the garden, God brought death into the world. It is a fact that we all are going to die someday. It was planned as part of our lives from the day we were born. You don't like it, but that's the way it is. It shouldn't be *dreadful*, but *delightful* because of what awaits us in heaven.

II. Death is Peaceful
For the children of God, death should be peaceful. There have been people we have met who knew they are going to die and who found peace because their spirit bears witness with God's spirit. They knew that soon they will be in heaven and meet Jesus. We still want to stay here, but someday all our families and friends will die as well. If they are children of God, we will spend eternity together in heaven with them.

III. Death is Purposeful
There is a purpose in death as well. That purpose is for us to be a witness to others so they can see Christ in us and the peace that we have at that time. If they need to be saved, it can be an example for their need for Christ. It can also help other believers to see death as peaceful and purposeful as well. That should be our purpose, both in life and in death.

APPLICATION: If you know someone who is terminally ill, pay him or her a visit. Read scriptures on the purpose of death for the Christian, and witness to them if they are not a believer. This again is a large part of our purpose as a believer.

WEEK 5—THURSDAY

A *Serving* Leader

SCRIPTURE READING: Nehemiah 5:14–19
THREE KEY WORDS: Service—Sacrifice—Surrender

I. **Service**
One of the main characteristics of a good leader is the fact that he is willing to serve others before he serves himself. One of Zig Ziglar's famous sayings is, "You will get everything in life that you want if you will help enough other people get what they want." As that quote says, leaders who serve will serve as good leaders. Jesus said, "I came not to be served, but to serve," and He was the greatest leader who ever lived.

II. **Sacrifice**
A good leader is also willing to sacrifice himself for the good of others. This is just like Nehemiah. He didn't take a salary because they had no money. He wouldn't eat or allow his other key people to eat special food. They ate what the workers ate. He didn't supervise the building of the wall; he got on the wall with his people and worked. He led by example, and we should do the same.

III. **Surrender**
To be an effective leader, we must also surrender everything to the Lord and let Him lead us in everything we do. We must have the wisdom from God to be an effective leader, and the rest will follow. There's a famous saying that says, "Lead by example and judge by results." An effective leader will do just that.

APPLICATION: Today, as you go to your job or be with family and friends, show the strongest leadership characteristics by being a serving leader. Ask those around you what you can do special for them to help them that day. Don't take "no" for an answer. Do something good for someone today.

WEEK 5—FRIDAY

Do Not Lie to Others

SCRIPTURE READING: Colossians 3:3–19
THREE KEY WORDS: Lying—Living—Loving

I. **Lying**
God clearly tells us in His Word to not to lie to others. In fact, it is one of the Ten Commandments. However, in a *USA Today* article, it stated that ninety-one percent of people lie about small things, and seventy percent lie to their wives and kids. The only reason we lie is to make an impression on others or get ourselves out of a jam. God clearly says, "Don't do it." You cannot cover up something because God knows everything there is about us anyway. The best thing we can do is to always be truthful.

II. **Living**
God says we are living a new life since we were saved. We are continually growing in our walk with the Lord, and part of our growing process is to be more like Christ. When Christ was here on earth, He never sinned, which means He never lied. He is an example for us because He was always truthful. The Bible says we have the mind of Christ—therefore, if we have the mind of Christ, we have the power of Christ as well, and we can always be truthful.

III. **Loving**
Since Christ loved us so much that He died for us, His Word says that love should guide our lives more than anything. He also says we are to practice tenderhearted mercy and kindness towards others like He did for us. One of the ways not to show your love is to lie to someone or about someone. I've heard it said that if you tell people to lie for you, they will lie to you. So one of the characteristics of love, as Jesus says, is truthfulness at all times.

APPLICATION: Make a commitment today, and every day, that no matter what happens, you are going to be truthful. This also means you will not exaggerate as well. Also, if you have not been truthful to someone, go to that person, make it right, and ask for forgiveness.

WEEK 6—MONDAY

From *Servant* to Savior

SCRIPTURE READING: Philippians 2:1–11
THREE KEY WORDS: Reputation—Rights—Reign

I. Reputation
God was not making a reputation for Himself when He left heaven and came to earth as a servant. He could have been the most popular king who ever lived. There have been many kings, but there is only one God. The King Jesus was rejected, ridiculed, and had no reputation from the people at the end. Don't build your life to be a somebody, but build it to serve the King.

II. Rights
Jesus did not choose His rights as God. He laid aside his rights and reputation to be a humble servant and to serve others. Most kings want to be served, but the greatest King of all came to serve others. We should lay aside our rights many times so we can serve others as well.

III. Reign
Although Jesus laid aside His reputation and rights to serve others, the truth of the matter is that someday He will reign as the King of Kings and Lord of Lords. If we are born again, we will also reign with Him forever. That is the most important thing we have to look forward to, spending eternity with our King.

APPLICATION: To be an effective follower of the King, we must not worry about our reputation among others in doing so. We have to lay aside our rights, not only to be a follower, but to lead others to the King. Make that commitment today.

WEEK 6—TUESDAY

Who Controls Your Plans?

SCRIPTURE READING: Proverbs 16
THREE KEY PHRASES: Controlled Plans—Changed Plans—
Committed Plans

I. **Controlled Plans**
We develop our plans for life, and we believe the only way these plans can come to pass is to set goals and stay in total control of our own lives. We must realize that God has a perfect plan for our lives, and He wants us to yield the control to Him.

II. **Changed Plans**
Many times our plans are going to change. We will have new opportunities in our lives, and it may require a move to a new location like it did for me many years ago. If we are in tune with God's will, we will accept that even the changed plans are a part of His plans. This is true in my life and in the lives of many others as well. God moved me to Dallas for a reason, and then to Denver. If our plans are changed by God, they are changes for the better.

III. **Committed Plans**
God wants us to let go of the control button of our plans and commit everything we do to Him. Commit our plans to the Lord, and He will direct our paths. This is hard to do, but it is the only way we will succeed. I recently heard a quote that said, "Set your goals in pencil, and then give God the eraser." Good advice.

APPLICATION: In your prayer and Bible reading, tell God that from this day forward you are putting Him in charge of your plans. Then ask Him for strength to accept any changes He might have for you in your future. There is an old saying, "Let go and let God." Make that your commitment today.

WEEK 6—WEDNESDAY

Your Greatest Legacy—Greatest Inheritance

SCRIPTURE READING: Deuteronomy 6:1–9
THREE KEY PHRASES: Lasting Legacy—Loving Legacy—Lifelong Legacy

I. Lasting Legacy
We must remember that as we work to build our future that our legacy when we die will not be based on what we have: our wealth, *possessions*, *positions*, or *prosperity*. Our legacy will be based on how our families remember us and our eternal accomplishments. As Proverbs says, "Have one goal—common sense and a good reputation."

II. Loving Legacy
The best legacy to leave our kids is to love God and to love and be faithful to our spouses. The best legacy we can leave our grandchildren is to love our children unconditionally. They must see that we love God more than anything else and that we are a spiritual example in everything we do.

III. Lifelong Legacy
Fifty years from now, the way we will be remembered will be by what we did for God, family, and friends. My favorite quote is, "Fame is a vapor, popularity is an accident, money has wings. Those who cheer you today will curse you tomorrow. The only thing that endures in life is our integrity and character." Ironically, this was quoted by O.J. Simpson in his Hall of Fame speech. Leave a legacy of integrity and character, which will always be remembered by the ones who love you most.

APPLICATION: Whenever temptation that could affect our legacy comes along, remember the above-mentioned quote and the people in business, ministry, and politics that violated their integrity. Look at their consequences and then ask yourself, "Is it really worth it?"

WEEK 6—THURSDAY

How Do You View God?

SCRIPTURE READING: Exodus 24
THREE KEY PHRASES: God's Presence—God's Purity—God's Purpose

I. God's Presence
Paul said in 1 Timothy 6:15 that we can't physically see God. God's spirit is present everywhere we look. We can see His creation, His miracles, and His working in our lives. We need to take time to see God's presence in our lives and His working with us daily. His Holy Spirit is in us and present everywhere we go.

II. God's Purity
Jesus said in Matthew 5:8, "Blessed are the pure of heart, as they shall see God." One of the requirements for us to see God, and His presence working in our lives, is to be pure. God said there should be no idols in our lives. If we are not pure in mind and in heart, then we have an idol that is more important than God. We have to work daily to stay pure in heart to experience God's presence.

III. God's Purpose
God has a purpose our lives, and He wants us to stay pure so we can feel and experience His presence so He can carry out that purpose. We need to pray daily that God will give us the strength to do so.

APPLICATION: In today's world, with all the sin of immorality, we have to pray daily that God will give us a pure mind and heart. There is nothing like the freedom of God working daily in our lives. Surrender your heart and mind daily to God to stay pure so you can experience His presence and fulfill His purpose.

WEEK 6—FRIDAY

Are You Ready?

SCRIPTURE READING: Luke 12:34–39
THREE KEY WORDS: Ready—Return—Reward

I. **Ready**
   Just as we get ready every day to go to work, get ready each year for a new year, get ready for our retirement, Christ said we are always to be ready for the greatest event that will ever take place, His return. To be ready, we must be saved and also live our daily lives like He might come today, because He might.

II. **Return**
   Christ said that He will return. That is a promise. He said, "I don't know when, but someday the Father will tap me on the shoulder and say, 'Son, it is time for you to go get my family and bring them home. I am ready for them to return. Go and get them.'"

III. **Reward**
   When Christ returns to us, we will go to heaven to get our reward. In verse 37 it says that there will be great joy. He Himself will put on a waiter's uniform and serve me. Oh, what a promise. Oh, what a Savior. We need to do our best to be ready at all times.

APPLICATION: As you begin your day, give yourself a checkup from the heart up to make sure you are ready. If you are not, then get on your knees this minute and make it right in order to be ready. This might be your day.

WEEK 7—MONDAY

Vengeance is Not Mine

SCRIPTURE READING: Roman 12:14–21
THREE KEY WORDS: Vengeance—Vendetta—Violence

I. Vengeance
It is a fact that people in life are not always going to be good to us. Those same people, even our Christian brothers and sisters, are going to do us wrong. This can hurt us more than them if we let it make us bitter, or it can make us better if we live by the scripture that says, "Vengeance is mine, says the Lord. I will repay them." So let God do it.

II. Vendetta
When we try to do things ourselves it becomes a vendetta against others that can destroy friendships. My mom and dad are good examples of that. Because of a vendetta my mom had against my dad's family, it ended up hurting a lot of people, and it always will. As a result, my parents divorced after thirty-eight years of marriage, which destroyed our family.

III. Violence
The result of vengeance and vendettas may turn into violence that can lead to devastation. People have been hurt and killed because they took matters into their own hands. God says not to let evil get the upper hand and conquer *vengeance, vendetta,* and *violence* by doing good and turning it over to God and letting Him handle it His way. This is the true way to handle vengeance.

APPLICATION: If there is someone in your life today who you hold a grudge or bitterness towards, just surrender it to God and let Him handle it. I can guarantee you that a big weight will be lifted from you and your joy will return. Ask God to do it today.

WEEK 7—TUESDAY

Bad Things Happen—What Do We Do?

SCRIPTURE READING: 2 Corinthians 4:1–18
THREE KEY WORDS: Despair—Doubt—Defeat

I. Despair

Paul had a lot of discouragement and despair in his ministry, but he never gave up. When we get discouraged in our work, and see no light at the end of the tunnel, like Paul we need to look to our Father and Brother to deliver us through their strength and power, and not our own. Things are going to happen, and we must turn them over and let the Lord handle them.

II. Doubt

Sometimes I get so discouraged that I have doubt if I am going to make it or not. I am ashamed to say that sometimes in the past I have even doubted my salvation, but that is what Satan wants us to do. Don't ever doubt that Christ is there. I wouldn't be witnessing or writing this if He wasn't in my heart. These things I write that you may know that you have eternal life.

III. Defeat

When we feel like we could be defeated, like Paul said, "Never give up." In verse 18, Paul says, "Don't look at all the troubles that we can see right now, but look forward to the joys in heaven that we have not yet seen. The troubles will soon be over, but the joys to come will last forever". Hang in there.

APPLICATION: If you are facing depression or doubt today, remember that greater is He that is in you, than He who is in the world. Tell Satan to back off and declare victory through the blood of Jesus. Your *despair* and *doubt* will become *delightful* because you *defeated* the evil one.

WEEK 7—WEDNESDAY

When God Seems to be Absent

SCRIPTURE READING: Job 23:1–12
THREE KEY PHRASES: God's Absence—God's Awareness—God's Answer

I. God's Absence

Sometimes when problems come into our lives, we think God has forgotten us or that He has abandoned us. Job thought that. He said, "I search in vain. I seek Him, I cannot find Him. It feels like He has hidden Himself from me." That is the way we sometimes feel, that we are empty, God is absent, and nowhere around.

II. God's Awareness

Job said that even though we feel like God is not there, He is always present. In verse 10 he said that God knows every detail of what is happening to us. He has a purpose for you and me, and whatever He wants to do, He does. So He will do for me all that He has planned. We have to realize that whether things are good or bad, God is always with us.

III. God's Answer

God says in his Word that He will never leave you nor forsake you. He is a friend who sticks closer than a brother. Job said, "If I go to His throne, He will not overpower me with His greatness, He will listen with sympathy." No matter how tough it gets, God is always with us. Never forget that.

APPLICATION: If you are feeling lonely, empty, or helpless today, read the entire book of Job and then be thankful that you haven't had to go through all of his pain. Also, remember the promise of God, that His understanding is unlimited. Ask Him for His awareness in your life today.

WEEK 7—THURSDAY

When Tragedy Strikes—Worship

SCRIPTURE READING: Job 6
THREE KEY WORDS: Winds—Worship—Winning

I. Winds
When the storms of life come our way, we are not supposed to abandon God, but we are to acknowledge Him and be aware of Romans 8:28. Look at the storm that Job faced in chapter 6. He didn't have a pity party and turn away from God. He turned to God in thanksgiving and said, "The Lord gives and the Lord takes away. Blessed be the name of the Lord."

II. Worship
When we face the wind in the storms of life, turn to God in worship. In the presence of Jehovah, troubles vanish, and hearts are mended in the presence of the King. Job said, "Blessed be the name of the Lord." He never second-guessed God. Worship gives us strength.

III. Winning
When the winds come through, the formula for us is to not fight the battle, but do as God says. "Cast all your cares upon Him, because He cares for you." When we face the wind, let God take control and worship Him for the victory that will be won.

APPLICATION: Remember, the Bible says, "The battle is not mine, but God's." No matter how big the storm, God can control the fiercest wind. Take time right now and just surrender your storm and tragedy to God, and ask Him to give you perfect peace. It all begins with you.

WEEK 7—FRIDAY

Free at Last, Free at Last

SCRIPTURE READING: 1 Corinthians 6
THREE KEY PHRASES: Forgiveness of Sin—Freedom from Sin—Future Without Sin

I. Forgiveness of Sin

We come into the world sinners. The Bible says, "In my mother's womb, I was formed in sin." We get trapped by sin, and it controls us. But Jesus came and died on the cross, and when I accepted Him as my Lord and Savior, He forgave all past, present, and future sins. What a blessing.

II. Freedom from Sin

Paul says that we are now free from sin. We have new desires, not to let sin control us. By grace we can do anything we want, but our wants should change. Be careful or you will get trapped. He also says that sexual sin is never right. We are joined to Christ, and we cannot join ourselves to Satan by sexual sin. We are free from that by the spirit living in us.

III. Future without Sin

Some day we will go to heaven and live forever. There will be no more sin, no more temptation, and no more giving in. We'll be totally free from Satan and all the things he has brought against us in the past. Praise God for this wonderful promise.

APPLICATION: No matter how bad we have been in the past, and no matter what may happen when we stumble in the future, God freed us forever by forgiving our past, present, and future sins. Everyday, thank Him for His forgiveness, and claim your freedom from the evil one. Then go forth and have a great day.

WEEK 8—MONDAY

Soil

SCRIPTURE READING: Luke 8:3–15
THREE KEY WORDS: Soil—Seeds—Success

I. Soil

Our hearts are like soil. We constantly need to take care of our hearts like soil. We need to keep God's Word in our hearts, watering and fertilizing it so it will grow. We can't let the ground get hard, and we must fight the devil and not let our heart get hard. We must do this in order to have good soil.

II. Seeds

After we have prepared the soil, we plant the seeds of God's Word in our heart daily. We must water, fertilize, and prune our hearts so the seeds of God's Word will grow. Then we can grow close to Him. Just like the Chinese bamboo tree, which must be watered and fertilized daily for five years before it grows, we cannot miss a day of watering and fertilizing the seeds in our hearts, or they will quit growing.

III. Success

Just like the farmer will see a harvest if he is faithful at taking care of his soil and seeds, so we will be successful in reaping a harvest from God's Word by taking care of our soil and seeds. It is something we have to work on constantly to keep our hearts from getting hard.

APPLICATION: As you pray and read God's Word daily, ask Him for a soft and tender heart to receive the seed from His Word. Throughout the day, water that word by meditating on it and applying it to your life as well.

WEEK 8—TUESDAY

What's Happening?

SCRIPTURE READING: Matthew 15:1–20
THREE KEY PHRASES: Unclean Hearts—Untrue Hearts—
Understanding Hearts

I. Unclean Hearts

Sometimes people walk up and simply say, "What's happening?" What they really mean sometimes is, "What is going on in your life?" Jesus told the Pharisees that it wasn't the food that they ate that caused unclean hearts, but what they think and say that causes them to be unclean. The heart is what produces unclean thoughts, causing us to think or say unclean words. So, what's happening? It all depends on our hearts.

II. Untrue Hearts

Like the Pharisees, we can pretend to be righteous or that our hearts are right with God. But the Bible says that God knows our hearts and we cannot fool Him. In today's world, in all the uncleanness around us, we must let God's Word change our hearts and ask Him to give us the power and desire to be clean and true to Him and for Him.

III. Understanding Hearts

We must understand that what we put into our minds is what affects our hearts. The Bible says, "what a man thinks in his heart, so he is." I've often asked myself how do we think with our hearts, and then I realized that what goes into our minds is what affects our hearts. To understand God's purpose and will for our lives and to understand the needs of others, we must have clean and truthful hearts. We need to get our heart right with God daily.

APPLICATION: Every morning when you pray, confess the sins in your life in order to have a clean heart. Just like a good shower cleanses us on the outside, a good time of confession will cleanse us on the inside. Then we will understand God's Word and the needs in other people's lives to the fullest.

WEEK 8—WEDNESDAY

Why Should We Praise God?

SCRIPTURE READING: Job 38:1–18
THREE KEY PHRASES: God's Majesty—God's Message—God's Miracles

I. God's Majesty

Like Job, we get so busy that we forget how majestic God really is. He reigns daily on high. He created me in a wonderful way, and every morning when I wake up and look out my window to see the sunrise, the beautiful mountains, the beautiful deer walking on the golf course, and hear the sounds of the birds, I should stop and praise God for all His wonders and beauty, and especially the majesty in everything He does.

II. God's Message

Like Job, when things get tough, we may even doubt God, but God's message is before us every day in His beautiful creations—the sunrise, the mountains, the ocean, the snow, the rain, and the animals, such as the beautiful sights and sounds of birds. His knowledge is a message to us that He is there and in control of everything.

III. God's Miracles

We must never forget the miracles of salvation through the birth, death, and resurrection of God's Son, Jesus Christ, who went to the cross and died for us so we could escape hell. What a miracle. Lord, help us never to forget and always help us remember to praise you daily.

APPLICATION: As you start your day, take just a moment to look around you and see God's presence through all of the wonderful things in His creation. Remember His miracles, and then take time to praise Him.

WEEK 8—THURSDAY

Don't Interrupt Me

SCRIPTURE READING: Mark 5:21–43
THREE KEY WORDS: Inconveniences—Individuals—Introspection

I. Inconveniences
When we go through our day, our routine, and our work, there are many inconveniences. We get stuck in traffic, we have trouble with our cars, we receive interrupting phone calls, people drop by to visit, and problems pop up at home. Our lives are filled with inconveniences, but nobody had more inconvenience than Jesus did Himself, but He always found time for the important things, the people.

II. Individuals
As we go through our busy days, we have many individuals who come into our lives. They're all hurting like the people who came to Jesus. Jesus was never too busy for someone in need, whether it be a little child, or a leper, or Mary and Martha with Lazarus. He always had time, and we need to take time to do the same. We need to listen to and encourage others.

III. Introspection
We also need to take time to look inside ourselves and ask if we really have compassion like Jesus had. You might be hurting for fellowship and friendship. Go and show compassion for others, and go be a friend to someone today. A famous doctor once said that if you are depressed and want to overcome your depression, go find someone else who is depressed and help him or her to overcome their depression, and yours will go away as well. That's what we need to do when helping others.

APPLICATION: As you go through your busy day today, if someone comes to you and has a need, be like Jesus and take time to listen. Look inside yourself and do whatever is necessary to show compassion to that person. That is what Jesus would do.

WEEK 8—FRIDAY

Listen to Others

SCRIPTURE READING: Psalm 18:1–6
THREE KEY PHRASES: God Knows Me Personally—God Feels My Pain—God Hears My Prayers

I. God Knows Me Personally
In my praise book this morning, it said that God created me as one of his jewels, flawless and clear. I am one of His spiritual masterpieces. Therefore, God knows me personally and wants only the best for me. He wants me to walk with Him daily and realize that He's there as my Father to love me and take care of me.

II. God Feels My Pain
Every time I hurt, God knows it. Like David, I feel the floods of ungodliness mounting a massive attack against me. I am so weak from the battle sometimes, but like David, I must realize that God is my fort where I can enter and be safe. He is the rugged mountains where I can hide. He is my Savior and shield and He wants me to bring my pain to him.

III. God Hears My Prayers
Distressed, David screamed to the Lord for help, and his cry reached heaven and the Father heard his prayers. They reached His ears and He answered. God, today I am screaming for help with the war of the flesh and spirit, and also with what to do for the future. Please help me today and answer, I pray. God listens when we scream out to Him when we are hurting, like He did for David.

APPLICATION: No matter how big God is, He always has personal time for us. If you are suffering from physical, emotional, or spiritual pain, just go to God in prayer and cry out to Him. He will personally come and help you. How awesome is that?

WEEK 9—MONDAY
Christian Life

SCRIPTURE READING: Acts 20:22–35
THREE KEY WORDS: Tough—Task—Truth

I. Tough

There's an old adage that says, "If it were easy, everybody would be doing it." That is one of the reasons that some people don't want to be Christians. It is really tough to live for Christ. Many preachers today teach that it is easy, but if you look in the Bible, all of the great people had it tough, including Christ Himself. It is hard to take a stand for what you believe. It is hard to lead a pure life, but even though it is tough, when we are tough on ourselves, it will become easier for us.

II. Task

To be an effective Christian, we must do daily tasks as a Christian. That includes time in prayer, time in God's Word, and time to minister and encourage others, and to tell others about Christ. In our daily busy schedules, it is tough to find time to do this, but we must do so.

III. Truth

If you are going to walk and live in the truth of God's Word, it will be tough. No matter how tough it gets, we will triumph if we are faithful. We will receive our trophy from Christ Himself when He says, "Well done, good and faithful servant. Enter into the kingdom of God." It is tough, but it will be worth it.

APPLICATION: Make a commitment that from this day forward you are going to be tough-minded about your Christian walk, then set out and do the task that God wants you to do today.

WEEK 9—TUESDAY

Never Doubt Christ Coming

SCRIPTURE READING: 1 Thessalonians 5:1–11
THREE KEY WORDS: Coming—Certain—Close

I. Coming

Christ is coming. Jesus said in John 4:13, "I am going to prepare a place for you and I will come again to get you so that you may be with me forever." Throughout the Bible there is a lot of prophecy, including Jesus's birth, death, and resurrection, which have already been fulfilled. There is also much written about His coming and the events leading up to this. If we think about these things, it should give us hope for the future.

II. Certain

Christ's coming is also certain. Throughout the New Testament there is a lot of evidence leading up to His coming. These again are events that will lead up to His return. The Bible is truth now and the one truth for the future. The second coming of Christ is just as certain as the sun coming up in the east and setting in the west.

III. Close

Christ's coming is also close at hand. Jesus said that no one knows the time of His coming. Only the Father knows, but there will be signs of His coming. If we look at the world events taking place today, they point to the fact that the coming of Christ is not only certain but it is close. Be ready at all times.

APPLICATION: Christ is coming soon, no doubt about it. Think of family, friends, and neighbors who you want to see go with you when Christ returns. Make a commitment to Christ that you will be ready, but also that you are going to help other people get ready by winning them over to the Lord as well.

WEEK 9—WEDNESDAY

Can't Fake It

SCRIPTURE READING: 1 Kings 12:1–10
THREE KEY PHRASES: Rationalizing Sin—Responsible for Sin—Repenting of Sin

I. Rationalizing Sin

When we are not in close fellowship with God, we can fall into temptation. As the Bible says, God does not tempt us. We are all tempted by our own thoughts and enticements, and if we are not careful, we can fall into sin. Sometimes we enjoy the sin so much that we rationalize that it is okay. We live under grace, but grace is never a license to sin.

II. Responsible for Sin

As Christians, we are responsible for our own actions. We live in a world today that is filled with temptations, and we must be strong or we will fall into sin. If we do, we make the choice, not God, not Satan, but us. Satan will tempt us, but we will make the choice to sin. We are responsible.

III. Repenting of Sin

Because we are responsible, we can't fake it to make it to heaven. We must repent and be born again. After we are born again and we sin, it is reassuring to know that no matter how far we go into sin that 1 John 1:9 says, "If we confess our sins, He is faithful and just to forgive us of sin and cleanse us from all unrighteousness." That's a glorious reassurance that He is faithful and forgives us no matter what.

APPLICATION: Realize that if we have unconfessed sin in our lives, we cannot rationalize it. We are responsible for it, and we must get on our knees and repent. After we confess our sin, we should get a partner to hold us accountable and responsible for the future.

WEEK 9—THURSDAY

How Do You Influence?

SCRIPTURE READING: 1 Timothy 2:1–7
THREE KEY WORDS: Power—Purpose—Prayer

I. Power
We have the power to be a good or bad influence on others. As I talk to other people, they tell me that I have been a powerful influence on them. One of my best buddies, John, told me that I was the most powerful spiritual influence on his life. That is why I should do my best every day and that I should realize that I can't "blow it" at this point, because if I do, all that powerful influence has gone by the wayside.

II. Purpose
Paul said that his only purpose in life was to please the Father. We should have that same purpose. We should love others so much and want to keep them out of hell that our purpose should be to tell others daily about the love and forgiveness of Christ. Then they can influence others for heaven as well.

III. Prayer
The only way we can have that power and purpose is through strong prayer. We must ask God daily to help us to defeat Satan who attacks us, to fill us with the Holy Spirit, and to live more in that spirit so we can be better witnesses for Him. It's not easy, but it should be a daily task for all Christians.

APPLICATION: Ask God to fill you with the power of the Holy Spirit today. Next, find someone you know, especially if they are a new Christian, and make the commitment that you will be a spiritual mentor and make an impact on their life. That will give you a new purpose daily.

WEEK 9—FRIDAY
Today's World

SCRIPTURE READING: Mark 8:1–9
THREE KEY WORDS: Changing—Caring—Compassionate

I. Changing

As I look back at my sixty-plus years and especially the last twenty-five years, things have changed so fast, but the greatest thing I see is the change in people. I remember when we used to get in the car and go visit some old friends of ours. We had time for the little things in life. I also believe that the people today don't have the convictions they once had to live for Christ. I know I do not myself, and that is sad. We live in a changing world, but God's Word never changes. He wants us to take time for others and also to keep our convictions.

II. Caring

We are so busy that we don't take the time to care for others. We don't listen or spend time with people who are hurting. There are people all around us who are hurting, dying, and going to hell. We must take time to care for our spouses, our children, our grandchildren, our neighbors, and all of our loved ones.

III. Compassionate

Jesus had compassion on the multitudes. He knew that they were hungry for physical and spiritual food. As we look at our fast-changing world today, we need to ask Jesus to give us more compassion for others to meet their hurting needs and to love them unconditionally. No matter how much we change or the world changes, we need to care and be compassionate. Those are the qualities that Christ had, and those are the qualities that we should have as well.

APPLICATION: One thing that never changes is the fact that people need people. There is no impact without contact. Think of someone you know who needs a personal contact, and then be caring enough to reach out and touch that person. You will be glad you did.

WEEK 10—MONDAY

Favor with God

SCRIPTURE READING: Titus 3:1–11
THREE KEY WORDS: Resentful—Reconciliation—Restored

I. Resentful

As we go through life, there are many different attitudes and choices we can make. When people treat us badly, we can become resentful. When we have something major happen in our life, we can even become resentful toward God, and we when we become bitter, we fall out of fellowship with Him. We can't live a life of "if only." If there's one thing I struggle with daily at my age, it is saying "if only," but I have to look forward.

II. Reconciliation

When we have hard feelings or are resentful toward one of our friends or family members, we can be reconciled to that loved one by asking their forgiveness and getting right with each other. In our married lives, we must do that many times with our spouses. The same is true with God. We need to reconcile our heart to Him whenever we feel like we are bitter or falling out of fellowship. That is the only way we can communicate with God.

III. Restored

When we ask forgiveness from God, and reconcile our hearts to His, God says in His Word that we are restored in fellowship with Him. We are His children and He is our Father, and in a parent-child love relationship, restoration is a great feeling. Unconditional love for each other is unbelievable. There is nothing like it.

APPLICATION: If we are resentful towards someone, or even God, the thing we must do is reconcile ourselves to that person and then to God. The Bible says that if we have resentment or hard feelings toward a brother or sister, we must go to them first, reconcile, and then we can be restored to God. Don't wait. Do it today.

WEEK 10—TUESDAY
Don't Be a Phony

SCRIPTURE READING: Isaiah 1:1–17
THREE KEY PHRASES: Imitation Faith—Insecure Faith—Influential Faith

I. Imitation Faith
The Israelites were not sincere about their faith, and it did not please God. We have to be sincere in our faith. We cannot go through the motions just to impress someone else. We must love the Lord with all our hearts and worship and praise Him sincerely. There's a statement that says that sometimes we are the best Bible that someone might ever read, and that comes from a strong faith, not an imitation faith.

II. Insecure Faith
If we are not sincere, we will become insecure. Is God really there? Am I really saved? Does God hear my prayers? Is God going to punish me? All of these things run through my mind. The one thing we need to remember is that God loves us and no matter what. We are His children. That is our security, not our insecurity.

III. Influential Faith
If we have a strong and sincere faith, we can influence others for Christ. We need to ask God to help us be a positive influence to others in our faith. He wants us to do so. We positively or negatively influence people. One of the ways we can positively influence is to have a godly, sincere faith.

APPLICATION: Due to some past mistakes by people in ministry, Christians have been labeled as imitations or insincere. We must be so sincere in our faith and so committed to God that our sincerity in our faith will be an influence on other Christians and the unsaved world. Make a commitment that you will be sincere as you daily walk in your faith.

WEEK 10—WEDNESDAY

The Importance of Being in the Right Place

SCRIPTURE READING: Esther 4:1–17
THREE KEY WORDS: Time—Talent—Truth

I. Time

As we study the Bible, God makes it very clear that He has made no mistake putting us where we are in this place of time. Time is of the essence, as God said there is a time to be born and a time to die. We only have so much time here on earth, and we are to use it for Him. Time is like a vapor, here today, gone tomorrow, so we need to make the best use of it every day.

II. Talent

Just like Esther, God has given us a talent. God has given me something special that I need to do, and He's done the same for you. He has given me the talent for telling my story, to teach, to witness, and to give. I need to surrender my total talent to Him to be used by Him for my time here on earth. God has a talent for you, but you need to find out what that talent is and use it.

III. Truth

The true fact is that some day we are all going to die and be judged by God. This is found in Hebrews 9:27, so how we use our time and talent for Him here will determine our rewards in heaven. Time is running out, so make every day count for Him. It will be worth it when we get to heaven.

APPLICATION: In this busy world, set aside some time each day to talk to God and ask Him to reveal the talent you have to use for His kingdom. When you discover that talent, set aside a couple of hours each week to use that talent for Him. It will be one of the greatest blessings in your life.

WEEK 10—THURSDAY

God is Holy

SCRIPTURE READING: Psalm 48
THREE KEY WORDS: Holy—Honest—Happy

I. Holy
We need to realize that our Lord and Savior is holy. He can't do anything that conflicts with His character, such as tell a lie or sin. He is perfect in His righteousness, truthfulness, and faithfulness. He cannot make a mistake. We cannot be perfect, but God wants us to try. He says, "Be holy, even as I am holy."

II. Honest
One of God's holy characteristics is honesty. He is honest in everything He says and does. Therefore, God wants us to be honest with Him first, and then be honest with everything we say and do, whether it is in our home, in our business life, or with friends or family; we are not to deceive others. Part of being holy is to be honest and truthful.

III. Happy
Another part of God's holiness is His perfect faithfulness. God will never let us down. His compassion for us is new every morning that we come to meet Him. He has a true love and compassion for us like no other, and this should make us happy. If we are happy and content with God, then we are successful.

APPLICATION: There is nothing like being holy and happy, and one of the keys to applying this is to be honest with both God and all others. We must surrender our hearts to God daily and ask Him to help us to be holy and acceptable to Him. This will bring us happiness and contentment as we walk in the fruit of the Spirit.

WEEK 10—FRIDAY
Joy and Peace

SCRIPTURE READING: Romans 5:1–10
THREE KEY WORDS: Power—Purpose—Peace

I. Power
In today's world, it is popular to have power and prestige, to work hard, go for the gold, and show everybody what you are made of. *Power, prestige,* and *popularity* are things we strive for in the workplace today, but that is not what brings us *purpose, patience,* or *peace*. These come only from God.

II. Purpose
God put us in this world for His purpose. His purpose is not to go after the worldly pleasures as mentioned above, but to have power through the Holy Spirit, prestige by being humble in spirit, and popularity, because you are now one of His special children. This will also give you a meaningful purpose by being a witness for Him.

III. Peace
People for centuries have searched everywhere for peace in drugs, sex, riches, and fame, but the only real peace comes from the relationship we have with the Father, Jesus our Brother, and the Holy Spirit. We need to turn everything over to Him, and when we surrender our will to His, we will find true joy and peace.

APPLICATION: We face all the temptations of the world every day in the marketplace. Remember, greater is He who is in you, than He who is in the world. Ask God to fill you with the power of the Holy Spirit so you experience peace throughout your day.

WEEK 11—MONDAY

Lessons of Life

SCRIPTURE READING: Ephesians 1:1–21
THREE KEY WORDS: Lessons—Listen—Love

I. Lessons

As we go through life, we learn many lessons the hard way. One of those lessons is to not to judge others. When we criticize or find fault with others, many times it is because we don't have all the facts. We prejudge, and that is sin, as God says not to do so. One of the best quotes I ever read was by Longfellow. It says, "Prejudging without thorough investigation is the height of ignorance." That's why we need all the facts.

II. Listen

If we feel critical of someone, we should do what the Bible says and go to them and ask for all the facts. Most importantly, we should really listen to what they have to say. It is also important to listen to the Holy Spirit. I have a definition for listening that says, "we listen to understand, not to replay." What is really being said to us between the lines?

III. Love

The Bible says that we should love our neighbors as ourselves; therefore, we need to learn to listen and to love unconditionally, with no strings attached. A great part of being loving is forgiving as Christ forgave us. A lesson to learn is to listen well and to love as Jesus loved.

APPLICATION: Decide today that you are not going to listen to gossip or prejudge others. Make a commitment that you will get all the facts and listen carefully before you draw your own conclusions. Then, no matter what, love others unconditionally.

WEEK 11—TUESDAY

The Sin of Immorality

SCRIPTURE READING: Proverbs 5
THREE KEY PHRASES: Danger of Immorality—Destruction of Immorality—Deliverance from Immorality

I. Danger of Immorality
As the Bible says, we need to watch for the sweet lips and beauty of an immoral woman. God says to run from her, and don't even go to the front door of her house. She really does not care for you, or the right path of life, so avoid her at all costs. God says don't expect for Him to help you to overcome temptation if you walk in the way of temptation. So we must avoid danger by avoiding the places we should not go to.

II. Destruction of Immorality
"An immoral woman is as destructive as bitter poison or a two-edged sword," says the Bible. Her feet go down to death. If we give into her, we will lose our honor and everything we have achieved in life. We will lose our wealth and health, and risk disease. We could face public disgrace if we give into immorality. The same is true for women as well as men. The Bible is very clear on this point.

III. Deliverance from Immorality
We first need to look to God for strength. God then says to drink from your own well. Share your love only with your husband or wife. Your spouse is like a loving deer, let them satisfy your every need, and be captivated by them. Most of all, remember the Lord clearly sees everything we do. This is too high a price to pay for immorality. If you don't believe this, look at all the people in business, religion, or politics that have been destroyed. Stay away from immorality and ask for God's help.

APPLICATION: As you pray today, ask God to put a hedge of protection around you as a protection against the dangers of immorality. If you are involved in immorality, ask God to deliver you and to save you from destruction. Through His love and power, you can be delivered.

WEEK 11—WEDNESDAY

Wisdom

SCRIPTURE READING: Proverbs 1
THREE KEY WORDS: Purpose—Problems—Punishment

I. Purpose
What is the purpose of wisdom? Wisdom is to teach us discipline, good conduct, and doing what is right and fair in all areas of our life, including friends, spiritual issues, finances, business, and raising a family. Wisdom is taking knowledge and applying it to everyday life. The fear of the Lord is the beginning of wisdom and life. It also warns us of the dangers of sin, running with the wrong people, and the consequences of doing so. Like a bird stays away from a trap, we are to stay away from people who might cause us to fall. Wisdom is critical, as it shows us how to live closer to God.

II. Problems
One problem is not applying wisdom as we should. When we don't apply wisdom, God says we become fools because we think we know it all. We become very narrow-minded. We live in the flesh and not in the spirit. Only God knows all. We are robbed of the pleasures of life that God has for us because of pride and greed. God says to humble ourselves under the mighty hand of God, and He will lift us up. If we apply wisdom, He will direct our paths.

III. Punishment
There is also some punishment for not applying wisdom. One of the punishments for not applying wisdom is living in sin. It is enticing and a quick route to prosperity and acceptance to people. When we go our own way, our appetite to satisfy sin becomes our master, and we will do anything to satisfy it. Even though sin looks good, it is deadly, and we need to learn that short-term pleasure causes long-term consequences. What a high price to pay for our own sinful moments of pleasure and the poison it brings into our lives and lives of others. Apply wisdom to carry out God's purpose.

APPLICATION: Make a commitment today that for the next thirty-one days you will read one chapter of Proverbs each day. It gives you purpose, helps you solve problems, and also avoid punishment. It has every answer you need for every area of life.

WEEK 11—THURSDAY

What Are We Seeing?

SCRIPTURE READING: Mark 14:1–9
THREE KEY PHRASES: Looking for Christ—Longing for Christ—
Loving Christ

I. Looking for Christ

In today's reading we learn that each of us see what we are looking for. As we go through life, our eyes reveal the desires of our hearts. Are we really looking to Christ, or are we looking to the pleasures of the world for satisfaction? Where your heart is, there your treasure will be also. The greatest pleasure we can find is looking for Christ and finding Him.

II. Longing for Christ

As we live our daily lives, we should have a longing to be like Christ and also a longing to walk in His will and have fellowship with Him. We should also have a longing to tell others about Christ and the price He paid to keep us out of hell. Our longing is to lead others to look for Christ and lead others to Christ as well.

III. Loving Christ

Christ should be the one we love the most in our lives. This is very hard to do sometimes, because it is hard to love someone we cannot feel or see. We should spend time with Him so we can learn to love Him more. Just as Mary showed her love through worship, we need to daily do the same. We do this through prayer and Bible study, and even by singing to Him as we have this time alone with God. As we start each day, we need to look for Christ, we need to long for His presence, and we need to love Him more than anything else.

APPLICATION: As you go out today, look for ways you can share Christ with others. Have a longing for a fellowship with Him. Also, love Him with all your heart so you can love your neighbor as you love yourself.

WEEK 11—FRIDAY

Friends

SCRIPTURE READING: Job 42
THREE KEY WORDS: Friends—Failings—Forgiveness

I. Friends

Job had a lot of friends when things were going well, like a lot of us do. When things got tough for Job, a lot of his friends left him, and three of them rebuked him, made fun of him, and accused him of sin while he was suffering. When times get tough, we need to be good friends more than ever. I heard it said once that we sometimes kill our wounded. Let that not be said of us as we befriend someone who is in trouble.

II. Failings

When times are rough, people will fail us miserably. If we need a loan, they don't have any money. When we need their time, they are too busy. This is why Jesus should be our best friend. He always will meet our needs during our toughest times. He said, "I will supply all your needs according to your riches and glory, by Christ Jesus." That includes our physical, financial, and emotional needs. Jesus is always there when you need Him.

III. Forgiveness

Just like Job, when our friends let us down and hurt us, we need to forgive them and pray for them. When we do that, God will bless us just like He did Job. We've let God down many times, but He always forgives us, and we should do the same for others. One of the greatest messages to come out of Job 42 says, "Because Job did this, God blessed him more than He ever did before."

APPLICATION: If you have a friend who is going through a tough time right now, remind that person of all his or her successes so that person won't focus on the failures. If someone has hurt you, forgive that person as God forgave you. That is the first step in receiving the blessings of God.

WEEK 12—MONDAY

God's Crossing in Life

SCRIPTURE READING: Psalm 77
THREE KEY PHRASES: Wading in Trouble—Work of God—Wonders of God

I. Wading in Trouble
When trouble comes our way and we don't see a way out, we need to focus on God and not ourselves. Asaph felt that way. He died because he doubted God's holiness and His love for him. Don't doubt God, and don't wade in the mud. Focus on Him to help you.

II. Work of God
When you feel doubtful, go back and remember all of the wonderful works God has done for you in your life. Think of His blessings, answered prayers, and just focus on Him. All you have to do is remember where you came from and where you are today. This is a miracle in itself.

III. Wonders of God
Think of all the wonders of God. Look at His creation. Look at all of the miracles in the Bible, and at all of the wonders in your own life. As we pray and worship, let's shift our eyes from ourselves to God and thank Him for everything.

APPLICATION: If you are going through a tough time right now, reflect back on what it was like before you became a Christian and how difficult it was without Him. Then, stop and thank Him that He is there to help as your Father through tough times. He will perform another wonder in your life that will get you through again.

WEEK 12—TUESDAY

God Always Forgives

SCRIPTURE READING: Mark 3:22–30
THREE KEY WORDS: Unforgiven—Understanding—Unbelievable

I. Unforgiven
Sometimes when I commit willful sin over and over again, I wonder if God will continue to forgive me. I even wonder if I am a real Christian. God says in His Word that the only sin that is unforgivable is blaspheming the Holy Spirit, the rejection of Christ, and who He really is. Many Christians worry about committing that sin, but do not need to.

II. Understanding
God understands everything we go through, but the proof of our salvation is our desire to know Him. If we go to Him every morning with a desire to know and praise God, then that is proof that His spirit lives within us, and even though it sometimes seems like we just go through the motions, we really do love Him.

III. Unbelievable
No matter how many times we sin or how we feel, our Father always forgives us. As His children, he takes us in His arms and tells us that He loves us. That is unbelievable. Thanks, Dad.

APPLICATION: Remember that God's understanding is unlimited. You cannot do anything so bad that He won't forgive you if you say that you are sorry. Remember also that He is "Abba Father," which means "Daddy." Thank Him for His unbelievable love and care for you.

WEEK 12—WEDNESDAY
Care for Others

SCRIPTURE READING: Ruth 2:1–13
THREE KEY PHRASES: Concern for Others—Caring for Others—
Communicate with Others

I. Concern for Others
As part of what we do daily, we need to care for others. People like us are hurting every day. They are lonely, discouraged, and are having a rough time of it. We should show genuine *concern* for them. Don't just do it in the flesh, but be sincere in your concern for others.

II. Caring for Others
Not only should we be concerned, but also should take care of people if we have the means to do so, just as Boaz did for Ruth. He not only cared for her with concern, but he also took care of her when he had her glean the best fields on purpose. Since he met a need of others, we should do so as well, because we really do care for them.

III. Communicating with Others
Some people just need a friendly word to meet their needs. One of the gifts God has given to us is the gift of encouragement, and it is a blessing to use that gift. We should give others a special greeting like Boaz did and make their day with a good word of encouragement. Lord, help us to do this daily.

APPLICATION: Ask God to show you a loved one or friend who has a real need. Be concerned and care for that person by meeting their needs. Whether it is financial, physical, mental, familial, or spiritual, make a commitment that you will meet that need.

WEEK 12—THURSDAY

Good or Bad Times

SCRIPTURE READING: Jeremiah 32
THREE KEY WORDS: Pain—Pleasure—Purpose

I. Pain
When we go through painful times in our lives, we always have God there to help us. Sometimes our pain is because we haven't turned to God in good times, and we forget Him. Life is tough and sometimes painful, but God is the great forgiver, physically and emotionally, so we need to turn to Him.

II. Pleasure
When things are really going well and we are enjoying all of the pleasures God is giving us, it is easy to forget that all pleasures come from God. We need to be so grateful and thankful to Him for all His goodness to us. Don't forget to worship and thank Him daily.

III. Purpose
God has a purpose for each one of us to grow through both our pleasant and our painful times. All things, both good and bad, work together for our good. We are to learn from both the good and the bad and use them to carry out God's purpose in our lives.

APPLICATION: To avoid going through spiritual pain, remember how wonderful it is with God in the good times and all the pleasures of living a Christian life. Then make it your purpose to daily do His will so you can enjoy these pleasures, and avoid the pain of not doing His will.

WEEK 12—FRIDAY

Hope

SCRIPTURE READING: Romans 8:18–27
THREE KEY WORDS: Hope—Help—Heaven

I. Hope
The Bible talks a lot about hope. In my daily life, I hope for a lot of things—that I can make it through another day, sell something, someday be closer to my family, and so on. Many days I frankly lose hope and don't think I can make it. But there are no hopeless situations. We only lose hope in certain situations. We should hope and rest in nothing less than Jesus and His righteousness.

II. Help
The Bible says when we have hope that God is our help in every time of need. He will never leave us or forsake us. With the Holy Spirit living in us, we can always turn to God for help and hope, but must surrender to Him completely to receive His help.

III. Heaven
Our greatest hope and help is heaven. God says that some day all of our problems will be solved when we get to heaven. There will be no sickness, death, loneliness, or sorrow. Heaven will only have beauty, happiness, and joy. We will be with Him and our loved ones forever. As Dr. Criswell used to say, "Look up, brother. Look up."

APPLICATION: If you have lost hope today, look to God. Ask Him for His help. Turn to scriptures that talk about heaven, then focus on these scriptures throughout the day.

WEEK 13—MONDAY

Sin Destroys Our Godly Attitude

SCRIPTURE READING: Matthew 5:1–12
THREE KEY PHRASES: Sadness of Sin—Sorrow of Sin—Solution to Sin

I. Sadness of Sin
When we look at what Christ says will make us happy, we are to be humble, meek, lowly, just, good, kind, merciful, and have pure hearts. We can lose it all by letting sin control our lives. The short-term pleasure of sin ruins the lifetime pleasures of happiness, because we let it control us. It is really sad that we let ourselves get in bondage to Satan.

II. Sorrow of Sin
To gain victory over sin, we must have godly sorrow. Look at the consequences of the short-term pleasure and see the sorrow in your loved ones' eyes. Ask yourself if it is really worth it. Look at all the people you know who have done this sin and the sorrow they have caused themselves and others, and then decide to do what is right.

III. Solution to Sin
If we are sad and sorrowful for what we do, the solution is to truly repent and give our hearts and lives to Christ. He is our only solution. If we can truly do this, we will be happy, because Christ will fill us with the attributes of the Spirit He talks about in Matthew 5.

APPLICATION: As you start your day, ask God to give you all the attributes of the Christian life He talks about in today's scripture. Cry out to God and be sorry for having committed willful sin, and ask God to forgive you. Then God will give you the joy and peace you need.

WEEK 13—TUESDAY

God's Wings

SCRIPTURE READING: 1 Peter 2:21–25
THREE KEY PHRASES: The Wings of God—The Workings of God—
The Wonders of God

I. The Wings of God
As a bird protects her little babies from harm by covering them with her wings, so God protects us by letting us take refuge under His wings. There is refuge and protection under the wings of God. We need to go there daily.

II. The Workings of God
As a bird works hard to protect her family, so God works with us to protect His family. He is always there to meet our needs. He takes all that we do and uses it for good so we can be closer to Him. We don't need works to save us, but we need to work daily to do our best to stay close to Him.

III. The Wonders of God
As a mother bird is willing to give her life for her little babies, God loved us so much that He gave us His Son to die for us, so that we could be protected from the evil one and have eternal life. This is so wonderful that it is very hard for us to comprehend. We need to focus on it daily and live for Him.

APPLICATION: As you begin your day, remember that God's wings are not only there to protect us but also to lift us up as we work for Him each day. If you get tired, ride on God's wings and then thank Him for all of His marvelous wonder.

WEEK 13—WEDNESDAY

Celebrate the Man

SCRIPTURE READING: 1 John 1
THREE KEY PHRASES: Real Man—Real Mercy—Real Message

I. Real Man
Young people today think that Walt Disney was just a name and not a real man. I sometimes have that problem with Jesus. I do not think of Him as God in the flesh, walking the earth, doing His ministry, and then dying for me. Jesus was God, but also a real man—the Son of God—and He lived among common people until He died for us. He is now in heaven with our Father, waiting for us some day.

II. Real Mercy
Jesus, our brother, had tender loving mercy for us and all the people with whom He came into contact. His mercy today is still the same, and it endures forever. Every day of our lives we need to focus on Jesus as a real man—our Brother. He loved us so much that He died for us.

III. Real Message
As Jesus' Brothers and Sisters we are to take the real message to others—that Jesus was born of a virgin, that He lived on this earth for thirty-three years, was a common carpenter until He began His ministry at age thirty, and He died on the cross for everyone so we could stay out of hell. We must believe this, and then go tell others.

APPLICATION: It is hard to be a real man or woman today as a Christian. Christ, however, is an example, so go out today and be Christ-like in everything you do.

WEEK 13—THURSDAY

The Gift of Thought

SCRIPTURE READING: Philippians 4
THREE KEY PHRASES: Terrible Thoughts—Terrific Thoughts—Trustworthy Thoughts

I. Terrible Thoughts

God has given us the gift of thought. A lot of animals are stronger and faster than us, but they don't have the gift of thought. There are terrible thoughts and terrific thoughts. If we don't discipline our minds, we can have terrible thoughts that cause terrible actions, especially immorality. As a man thinks in his heart, so he is. The mind is the gateway to the heart, and we reap what we sow.

II. Terrific Thoughts

Paul said to have terrific thoughts. Think about what is true, good, right, pure, and lovely. Look for the good in others. Think about all of the wonderful things you can praise God for and be thankful for with everything you do. Focus your thoughts on the cross of Christ and remember the terrific price He paid for us.

III. Trustworthy Thoughts

God says to "trust in the Lord with all your heart and lean not on your own understanding." This is true in our thought life as well. We must give our minds, hearts, and thoughts to God daily and trust Him completely. Do it every day.

APPLICATION: As you start your day and talk to God, ask Him to put a hedge of protection around your thought life. Put on the whole armor of God and use the helmet of salvation and the sword of the Word to defeat Satan. Trust God to give you pure thoughts today.

WEEK 13—FRIDAY

Refusing the Easy Way

SCRIPTURE READING: Daniel 1
THREE KEY PHRASES: The Right Path—The Right Purpose—The Right Prayer

I. The Right Path
The Bible says there is a path that seems right, but leads to destruction. As a river flows down the hill, it follows the path of least resistance. The same can be said of Christians. They fail to resist the devil, yield to temptation, and deviate from the path of God that we should follow. We can make sin flow easily if we flow like the river, or we can have the river of life if we stay on God's path.

II. The Right Purpose
Our purpose as Christians should be like Daniel's. We should have the purpose in our hearts not to defile ourselves. Our purpose is to be holy as God is holy and fill our lives with the Love of God.

III. The Right Prayer
The Bible says "greater is He that is in you than he that is in the world." We can be overcome or we can be overcomers by praying to God to give us a victory and stay on the right path. God, help us to have the purpose in our hearts to do so today and every day.

APPLICATION: God's purpose for the Christian is to stay on the right path, to live for Him, and to win others. As you start your day, pray for the necessary strength to do so, and then walk the straight and narrow path.

WEEK 14—MONDAY

Faith of a Child

SCRIPTURE READING: Matthew 18:1–10
THREE KEY WORDS: Forgetfulness—Forgiveness—Faithfulness

I. Forgetfulness

As we go though the game of life, we sometimes forget just how much our earthly fathers and our Heavenly Father really love us. When we do something wrong that hurts our fathers or makes them angry, we forget that they love us unconditionally. We are their children. True, they might get angry, but we must never forget their love for us.

II. Forgiveness

In today's scripture, Jesus says that no matter what we do, our Father will always forgive us. No matter how bad we have been or what we have done, all our Father wants us to do is simply say, "Father, I am sorry," and mean it. When we do that, forgiveness is immediate.

III. Faithfulness

We need the simple uncomplicated faith of a child to know that God forgives us. 1 John 1:9 says "if we confess our sins, He is faithful and just to forgive us and to cleanse us from all unrighteousness." Never forget that our Father forgives and is faithful to fix everything we have done wrong.

APPLICATION: No matter what takes place in your life today, remember that our *Father* is always *faithful* to *forgive* us because He loves us so much. Never forget.

WEEK 14—TUESDAY

The God of Hosea

SCRIPTURE READING: Hosea 1
THREE KEY PHRASES: Irrational Love—Interceding Love—Irrevocable Love

I. Irrational Love

When you read the story about Hosea and Gomer, it seems irrational that God instructed a man to marry a prostitute and to love her and be faithful to her, even though she was so unfaithful to him. However, it is just as irrational that God is always there to love us and to be faithful to us even though we are so unfaithful to Him daily. What a great illustration of love.

II. Interceding Love

God loves us so much that Jesus is interceding for us daily to our Father. Though we sin, He is forgiving us. This is Jesus's most important job; to intercede for us and to give us the power to be faithful to Him and the Father.

III. Irrevocable Love

No matter how bad we are, even living a life like Gomer did, God's love is irrevocable and cannot be changed. When we give our lives to Him, He said, "No matter what happens, I would never leave you or forsake you. I will always be there for you like I was for Hosea and Gomer."

APPLICATION: Sometimes when I start my day, I don't even feel like praying. My mind wanders, and I don't feel like my prayers even go out of the room, let alone to the throne of God. That is when I remember that the Bible says that Jesus is interceding for me. That seems irrational, but it is irrevocably the Love of Christ.

WEEK 14—WEDNESDAY

We Are Sojourners

SCRIPTURE READING: Colossians 1
THREE KEY PHRASES: The Tunnel—The Triumph—The Transition

I. The Tunnel
Sometimes life is like living in a tunnel. Things get dark and dreary. Problems overwhelm us, and there seems to be no way out. Sin makes our tunnel even darker. When we live in willful sin, Satan's darkness is horrible. This is what can cause life to be dark for us, but suddenly, through the Holy Spirit, we can see a light at the end of the tunnel. It is not a train going the wrong way; it is Jesus with His arms wide open waiting to help us.

II. The Triumph
Through Jesus and what He did on the cross, we can have victory over Satan and the darkness of life. The bright light of Jesus now lives in our hearts. That doesn't mean that we still won't experience darkness, but it does mean that the light of hope and the love through Christ is always there to help us.

III. The Transition
Some day we will transition from the tunnel of life on earth to the tranquility of joy and peace in heaven where there is no darkness, only pure beautiful light that we can enjoy for all eternity. If you are in the tunnel today, look to Jesus for your triumph.

APPLICATION: If you are in the tunnel of darkness today, study the scriptures. Next, look up the word "light" in your concordance, and read these scriptures as well. Then remember that you can come out and triumph over the tunnel of darkness by surrendering your day to Christ. Give it all to Him, and He will make your day brighter.

WEEK 14—THURSDAY

Possessions

SCRIPTURE READING: Philippians 3
THREE KEY WORDS: Earthly Possessions—Everlasting Possessions—Eternal Possessions

I. Earthly Possessions

We go through life totally working our fool heads off in order to get all of the earthly possessions we can. If we look in our closets, drawers, and garages, we have possessions that we always dreamed about, but we no longer even use or enjoy them. We think life is all about possessions, but when we get older, we realize the best things in life are not things. It is all a bunch of *junk*.

II. Everlasting Possessions

As Paul said in today's scripture, "I count all these possessions as nothing compared to knowing Christ." What is really important while we are here on earth is what we are doing to build everlasting possessions by pouring our lives into others. The most important possessions we have on earth are our *faith, family,* and *friendships.* What we leave behind to impact others for Christ is *jewelry*.

III. Eternal Possessions

As stated in the scripture today, our greatest riches we have are our riches in Christ. We strive for possessions here on earth, but some day we will have permanent possessions for eternity in heaven. God says, "I have a mansion just over the hilltop for you personally. That is reason for *jubilation*."

Application: People tell me all the time to take time to smell the roses. That is what God is saying here. Take time to invest in everlasting and eternal possessions, and don't work so hard for earthly possessions. You might not get a lot here, but you will have more than you ever dreamed of in heaven. Work for God today.

WEEK 14—FRIDAY

Spectator or Servant

SCRIPTURE READING: Hebrew 5
THREE KEY WORDS: Spectator—Servant—Surrender

I. Spectator
In the game of life, we sometime become spectators. We watch sports, people, and things just pass us by. In the Christian life, the same thing can happen. We just go to church and are spectators—no participation. We are looking for the good feeling, or we want to criticize what is happening. It is the old saying, "You only get out of something what you put into it."

II. Servant
Christ was not a spectator. He was a servant, and He wants us to be a servant as well. We should serve Him daily by reaching out to others, being obedient, becoming involved in church, studying His Word, and praising and praying to Him. Our service is important to Him.

III. Surrender
To do this, we must daily surrender ourselves. We must have a desire to serve Him and surrender our will to Him. We really need to do this no matter how we feel or what kind of mood we are in. Father, please help me be not a *spectator* but a *servant* by *surrendering* to You daily.

APPLICATION: The next time you go to church or read your Bible, simply surrender your time and heart to Christ. Participate in the worship service and sing as loud as you can. When the preacher is speaking or reading the Bible, ask God to speak to your heart. Next, ask God how you can serve Him in your church or personally to someone else. A spectator misses the blessings of being a servant to Christ.

WEEK 15—MONDAY
Straight Life

SCRIPTURE READING: Amos 7
THREE KEY PHRASES: Father's Plumb Line—Father's Punishment—Father's Principles

I. Father's Plumb Line
Just as a builder uses a plumb line to build a straight wall, so we as Christians must also use the plumb line of God's Word to build our lives and keep them straight. Just as a wall can get out of line, so can our walk with God if we don't walk the straight and narrow road that is God's road. The question we have to ask is, "How do we measure up to God's Word?"

II. Father's Punishment
Just like the scripture about the children of Israel, God will say enough is enough, and we will have to deal with His punishment. God has set the plumb line for us to follow, and if we love Him, we will follow it. The only reason God punishes is because He loves us. He knows we must walk the plumb line of life to be happy.

III. Father's Principles
God has set a blueprint for our lives just like a builder has a blueprint for a building. It is laid out in His Word. To have a solid foundation and to walk straight, we must daily check our plumb line.

APPLICATION: As you study the scripture for today, ask God to show you if there is anything out of line in your life right now that does not measure up to His Word or His will. Next, be committed to do your best to walk the straight and narrow for Him.

WEEK 15—TUESDAY
Seeds and Fruit

SCRIPTURE READING: Galatians 6
THREE KEY PHRASES: Seeds of Stress—Seeds of Sorrow—Seeds of Serenity

I. Seeds of Stress
As the scripture so adequately says today, we reap what we sow. Because I put pressure on myself, I daily sow seeds of stress. I hurry through the day and miss out on all the little things. I get frustrated, angry, unhappy, and quite frankly, tire myself out. I must change this pace so I can enjoy what God has for me.

II. Seeds of Sorrow
Because of my stress, I also sow seeds of sorrow. My flesh overtakes my spirit, and I do things I should not do and commit sin. It brings sorrow to my soul and also sorrow to my wife, as well as God. I treat her wrong because I sow seeds of sin. I need to lower my stress level, so I won't give into sin and be sorry, but if do, I need to be sorrowful and repent.

III. Seeds of Serenity
God says if we sow seeds of love and service and surrender to the Holy Spirit, He will give peace and serenity. All we need to do is surrender our will to Him. Starting now, I am going to sow good seeds to grow good fruit and to have a fabulous life. Help me, Lord.

APPLICATION: If we think we are going to avoid stress without God's help, it will never happen. To avoid *stress* that might cause us to give into *sin* that produces *sorrow*, *surrender* everything you do today completely to Him. If we do this, God will handle the *stress* that will prevent *sorrow* and give us *serenity* for the day.

WEEK 15—WEDNESDAY

Loneliness

SCRIPTURE READING: Psalm 34
THREE KEY WORDS: Loneliness—Learning—Loving

I. Loneliness
I think one of the hardest things in life to live with is loneliness. In my profession as a speaker, I get very lonely. I am in a car, on airplanes, in hotel rooms, and most of the time, all by myself. When traveling, I feel like I am cut off from the world. Many people suffer from loneliness—the widow, divorcee, the soldier. Loneliness is difficult.

II. Learning
Sometimes loneliness can be a learning experience. God sometimes puts us in the desert so we can see how much He really cares for us and that He is always there. He is a friend who sticks closer than a brother. No matter how lonely we sometimes feel, with Jesus we are never alone. His spirit is always with us.

III. Loving
When lonely, we must focus on the fact that God the Father, God the Son, and God the Holy Spirit love us more than anyone or anything in the world no matter what. We much look to heaven and say, "Someday I will never be lonely again. It will be worth it all when I get to heaven."

APPLICATION: If you feel lonely today, remember that your best friend in life, Jesus, is living in your heart. He is always with you. Also, if you are able, go to a hospital or nursing home and just be a friend to somebody. This will take your loneliness away.

WEEK 15—THURSDAY
Don't Play "What If?"

SCRIPTURE READING: Psalms 139
THREE KEY WORDS: Past—Present—Paradise

I. Past
One of the bad habits I have is living in the world of "what if?" or "if only." As we examine our past, we have all made mistakes, but we shouldn't let them paralyze our future. We should learn something from the mistakes we have made. We should be sorrowful and repent of all past sins, but the past is the past, so move on.

II. Present
We should live every day in the present. We should live it as if it were our last day, because it could be. We should live each day to the fullest, enjoy all the little things as well, and also live each day pleasing the Lord. The *present* will be *pleasant* if we *present* ourselves to Him daily and walk His *path*.

III. Paradise
With the past forgiven and our present secured, we also have paradise to look forward to. Just like the thief on the cross, someday we will be in paradise with Jesus. No matter what our past was, or our present circumstances are, it will be worth it when we see Jesus in paradise.

APPLICATION: If we can't do anything about yesterday, and we have no guarantee for tomorrow, then live this day to the fullest for God. Enjoy every moment with Him today, every tomorrow from this one on, and live one day at a time for sweet Jesus.

WEEK 15—FRIDAY
The Illusions of Life

SCRIPTURE READING: Malachi 3
THREE KEY PHRASES: The Illusions of Life—The Illustrations of Life—
The Infusions of Life

I. The Illusions of Life

An illusion is living in an unreal world. We see things that aren't real. We look at the world and its pleasures, and we see the great illusions of the enjoyment of sin. We hear, "Let's just party and be happy all the time." We think drinks, drugs, and sex are the answers to our happiness. That is what they thought in Malachi 3, but God abandoned them. Why? Because they left the real world of work and family for the illusion of sin and didn't think they were wrong.

II. The Illustrations of Life

God illustrates to us in His Word how the real world is. Life is not easy. It is tough, but if we abandon ourselves to God, He won't abandon us. He wants us to work hard, be faithful to our spouses and children, and most of all, be faithful to Him. He illustrated His love for us with the death, burial, and resurrection of Christ.

III. The Infusions of Life

God infuses us with power, joy, and happiness when we live in the real world of His illustrations. Satan tries to make all of those illusions look good, but in the end, they lead to destruction as it did in today's scripture. Stay in the real world by following God.

APPLICATION: Realize today as you walk with God that Satan is always trying to attack you with the illusions and pleasures of sin. Ask God to put a hedge of protection around you and to infuse you with His power to defeat Satan.

WEEK 16—MONDAY

God Sees

SCRIPTURE READING: Genesis 16
THREE KEY PHRASES: God Sees—God Solves—God Soothes

I. **God Sees**
God sees everything we do, both good and evil. We worry about what other people see, but we should strive daily to please God in everything we do because He sees us. Also, God sees our needs. He knows our problems, our hurts, and our sorrows. He sees our need for Him, and we need to seek Him as well.

II. **God Solves**
God will solve our problems and meet our needs if we will only let Him. There isn't any problem too small or too big for God. We just need to surrender them to Him. We need to quit solving our own problems and let God help us.

III. **God Soothes**
No matter how badly we may have been hurt, or lonely, discouraged, or in pain we are, God is there to comfort and soothe us. He says, "I will never leave you or forsake you." God not only hears us, He sees us and wants to soothe us, so surrender everything to Him.

APPLICATION: As you start your day, God sees and hears everything you do, say, and need. Therefore, do right all day. Turn your problem over to Him to solve; surrender everything to Him, and let Him soothe you all day long.

WEEK 16—TUESDAY

Words

SCRIPTURE READING: Romans 13:8–14
THREE KEY PHRASES: Gossip—Gentleness—Goodness

I. Gossip

In Proverbs it says gossip is that dish we most relish. Our tongues can destroy others. If I say "John is a jerk" to someone who hasn't met him, I have killed John with those words. We need to be very careful how we talk about others. Gossip is a hurtful sin, and we should work hard not to do it.

II. Gentleness

In dealing with people, we need to be firm but gentle. Harsh words and untrue statements can scar someone for life. The old saying "sticks and stones may break my bones, but words will never hurt me" is not true. Sometimes verbal abuse does more harm than physical abuse.

III. Goodness

The Bible says we can wrap up the whole law by loving our neighbors as we love ourselves. Be gentle and good to others. Be positive with your words and what you say. Don't be a gossip. Be a good-finder in others, and people will feel great for what you have done.

APPLICATION: Make a commitment today that you won't say anything bad about anyone else or listen to gossip. Be kind, gentle, and good when you talk to others today.

WEEK 16—WEDNESDAY
Finding the Truth

SCRIPTURE READING: *Colossians 2*
THREE KEY PHRASES: The Tales of Christ—The Truth of Christ—
The Teachings of Christ

I. The Tales of Christ
Many people today do not believe that Jesus led a sinless life or that He was raised from the dead. Many believe all religions are the same. Even some who call themselves Christians think this. There are many people who preach false doctrines about Christ being a good man, but these are all untrue and are tales.

II. The Truth of Christ
The fact is that Jesus was the Son of God, that He was born of a virgin, lived a sinless life, died on the cross, arose on the third day, and is coming back again. That is a fact and the truth of His Word.

III. The Teaching of Christ
To find this truth, we must share the Word and the teachings of Christ. All of the truth about Christ is in the Word, and the Bible says if you study the Word, you shall know the truth and the truth shall set you free. God is true to His Word.

APPLICATION: To be steady in the truth of God's Word, we must study His Word daily to receive the truth in our hearts. The more truth you know, the better equipped you will be to attack the false doctrines of the Word. Study God's truth daily.

WEEK 16—THURSDAY

Wise Counsel

SCRIPTURE READING: Luke 2:46–52
THREE KEY WORDS: Watching—Willingness—Wisdom

I. Watching

As we go through life, one of the ways we learn and also get wisdom is to watch others, especially older people. As I heard it said one time, if you want to be successful at something, find someone who is already a success at what you want to do, copy that person, and go do it. Then you will be successful, too. It has also been said that we are to be like a Bible that others read. We need to watch others in every area of life to learn from them.

II. Willingness

One other important thing in life is to be willing to learn. Proverbs says only a fool is not willing to learn. School is never out for the person who wants to be a pro at what they do. Proverbs says in 1:5 that "a wise man will hear and increase learning." We can never become so proud that we think we know it all. Be willing to learn.

III. Wisdom

Proverbs 1:5 also says a "man of understanding will attain wise counsel." Like Jesus, we need to increase in wisdom and stature to gain favor with God. One way to do that is to watch others and be willing to take advice.

APPLICATION: If you do not have an older person as a mentor, pray for God to bring one into your life. Meet with that person often. As the Bible says, "There is wisdom in a multitude of counselors." Also study a book in Proverbs daily to gain wisdom from God.

WEEK 16—FRIDAY

Our Legacy

SCRIPTURE READING: Psalms 46
THREE KEY WORDS: Life—Lord—Legacy

I. Life
There are many things in life we strive for, especially to please our children. We want to give them the best of everything, but the best thing we can give our children is a living example of the values and characteristics of Christ. When we leave this earth, the best present we can leave behind is an example they can follow.

II. Lord
To do this we must put the Lord first in our lives with everything we do, such as making decisions, raising our kids, and working at our job. We must always let the Lord be Lord of our lives. This is the only way we can be a living example to our kids and everyone we come into contact with. We need help every day to do so.

III. Legacy
The things we get for our children will get old and get put away, but the one thing that will last forever will be the legacy we leave behind—our living example of what we were and our love for them. Our love for the Lord is what will build our legacy.

APPLICATION: As we strive daily to make our mark in life, remember what the Bible says, "The only thing that we do for Christ will last. In everything you do today, do it as unto the Lord." That is the foundation for the legacy you leave.

WEEK 17—MONDAY

Weaknesses in Our Lives

SCRIPTURE READING: 2 Corinthians 1:1–10
THREE KEY PHRASES: Our Weaknesses—Our Wondering—Our Worthiness

I. Our Weaknesses

As we go through the game of life, we sometimes get weak and worn. As I hit the street every day, I get tired and weak. We have problems in our lives, like I did in business and with my children. Or you might have an illness, or you might be lonely. Sometimes we are so weak that every day we wonder if we can make it through another day. I feel that way often.

II. Our Wondering

Again, I sometimes wonder why God allows these struggles in our lives. I wonder if it is really worth it. Am I going to make it or throw in the towel? I wonder sometimes if I am really saved because of the sin present in my life. I wonder if I can even slow down and enjoy life, but ultimately all this wondering is what makes me weak.

III. Our Worthiness

Even while going through all of this, God says I am worthy. He says, 'Dave, just trust me. My grace is sufficient." He says I am an original masterpiece just like a great original painting. He also says that we are created in His image, so that in itself should make me feel worthy. He also says that worthy is the Lamb that was slain just for you and me. This sacrifice makes us worthy. What a price He paid for our worthiness.

APPLICATION: As you pray to God today, if you feel weak and worn, ask Him to give you the strength you need. Make a commitment not to ever quit, and also remember how worthy you are to Him.

WEEK 17—TUESDAY

Jabez

SCRIPTURE READING: 1 Chronicles 4
THREE KEY PHRASES: The Giver—The Gift—The Goal

I. The Giver
We must remember that God is the giver of all things in life. He gave us our health, our families, our homes, and all of the material blessings we have, but the most important thing God gave us was Jesus, our Brother. He died for us that we might have more abundant life here, but also that we might have eternal life as well.

II. The Gift
Everyone loves gifts, and that is why we should love God, because the greatest gift we will ever have is the gift of eternal life. God loved us so much that He gave His only Son to us that we could have the gift of staying out of hell and spending eternity in heaven.

III. The Goal
Our goal, because of the gift God gave us, is to honor God in what we do every day. Jabez was more honorable than his brothers. We should be honorable as well. God gave us the gift of life, and we should give that gift back to God every day to honor Him. Help us to do so.

APPLICATION: Thank and praise God for all of the wonderful gifts He has given you, but especially the gift of eternal life. Then set your goal today to honor Him in everything you do. It will make your day great.

WEEK 17—WEDNESDAY

What is a Life?

SCRIPTURE READING: John 20:11–18
THREE KEY PHRASES: The Past—The Present—The Promise

I. **The Past**
As we go through life, it passes by fast. We make mistakes, and some of us live in the past, like me, living the life of "if only." We all have made many mistakes in the past, but the past experiences can also be good. We can learn from those mistakes, and we also have had some wonderful things that have happened as well. Think on these things.

II. **The Present**
Today is the only day we have. Zig Ziglar says, "Yesterday is a canceled check. Tomorrow is a promissory note, so live this day to the fullest." No matter how tough it gets, enjoy the day. Take time to smell the roses. We should also do our best to live each day we have for Christ and for others.

III. **The Promise**
In today's scriptures, God has promised us a wonderful eternal life with Him and our loved ones because of the death, burial, and resurrection of Jesus. Don't be like Thomas and doubt it. Just believe it because it is real, and that promise will help us to live with our past and also enjoy the present day by day.

APPLICATION: Forget yesterday and focus on what you can do for Christ today. Spend some quality time with Him and focus on His promise of an *abundant* life on earth and an *awesome* life forever with Him in heaven.

WEEK 17—THURSDAY

Just the Facts

SCRIPTURE READING: Colossians 3
THREE KEY WORDS: Exaggeration—Examination—Expectations

I. Exaggeration

One of the things God does not want us to do is to embellish or exaggerate what we say. It always starts out as a little white lie, and before we know it, it is blown completely out of proportion. Depending on the story, it cannot only be hurtful to us and sometimes destroy us, but it can also hurt others deeply.

II. Examination

The Lord says, "Let a man examine his heart." We need to ask ourselves, "Why are we doing this? Why do we need to try to impress others? What benefit is it going to bring me What possible damage can it bring me? How is it going to hurt others? Is it really worth it?" Daily examination is important.

III. Expectations

As God said in His Word today, "Don't tell lies to each other." In our new life, we are to be Christ-like, and Christ never embellished or exaggerated anything. He was always honest and truthful, and if we are going to be like Him, we need to do the same.

APPLICATION: As you talk with people today, make sure not to exaggerate or embellish your stories. Examine everything you say before you open your mouth and ask yourself, "Am I building up or tearing down?" Build others up today, just like Jesus did.

WEEK 17—FRIDAY

Thoughts of Heaven

SCRIPTURE READING: Revelations 21:1–5
THREE KEY PHRASES: Our New Heaven—Our New Home—
Our New Happiness

I. Our New Heaven
Many people think of heaven as a bunch of angels in white robes flying around and sitting on clouds, but the Bible says that it has streets of gold, walls of jasper, and diamonds. It is a beautiful city, and it is a real place, just like earth. But nothing in heaven will rust away like on earth.

II. Our New Home
Before Jesus left this earth, he said, "I go to prepare a place for you, and if I go to prepare a place for you some day, I will come and get you and take you to that beautiful city and to your new home. In my Father's house there are many mansions, and I have one there just for you. It is something far more beautiful than anything you can imagine on earth."

III. Our New Happiness
God says we will be totally happy in our new home in heaven because He will be among us. Also, there will be no more sadness, tragedy, sorrow, or death. God will wipe away all of our tears. So stick with it here on earth; it will be worth it all when we see Jesus in our new home in heaven.

APPLICATION: There are days in this life where we have to face unhappiness. It could be from a broken relationship, sickness, loss of a loved one, or any number of things. That is just part of life. If you are unhappy today, take time to meditate on your new home in heaven where God will make you happy again.

WEEK 18—MONDAY

God is Faithful

SCRIPTURE READING: Psalm 119:89–96
THREE KEY WORDS: Pain—Promise—Prayer

I. Pain
Many of us have pain in our lives right now. I have the pain of my future, and many of us have pain from our children not living for the Lord, pain of loneliness that is almost unbearable, and pain of struggling with sin. We all have a great deal of pain every day of our lives, but God has made us a promise.

II. Promise
With every pain there is a promise. My future—God says He has my future in His hands. My children—He says to train a child right and when they get older, they will come home. Loneliness—God says He will never leave you, never forsake you. Struggling with sin—God says greater is He that is in you than He who is in the world. Sickness—by His stripes we are healed. Finances—He promises He will supply all of your needs. God is faithful to His promises.

III. Prayer
The best way to share our pain and receive God's promise is through prayer. Prayer is designed for us to come boldly to the throne of grace and talk to God. He promises to listen and to also answer. When we share our *pain* and receive God's *promises* through prayer, then we should also give Him *praise*.

APPLICATION: If you are going through physical, emotional, or spiritual pain right now, just go to the throne and talk to God. He will listen. Then, open your Bible to the book of Job and read just a few verses. That will help bring your pain into perspective.

WEEK 18—TUESDAY

Being Realistic

SCRIPTURE READING: Psalm 27
THREE KEY WORDS: Worry—Wait—Worship

I. Worry
We must be realistic when we worry. Psalm 56:11 says, "In God I have put my trust. I will not be afraid." Yet even Paul had anxiety in his life. It is a common thing to worry sometimes. We all do it, but we must remember that verse because Satan wants us to worry, and really, the only way we can overcome worry is to put our trust in God.

II. Wait
Psalm 27:14 says "wait on the Lord, be of good courage, and He will strengthen your heart." The hardest thing for me to do is wait. It is something I don't like to do because I think I can handle everything myself, but I need to ask God for patience and wait for His answer. I need to wait for Him to tell me what to do.

III. Worship
The best way to overcome worry is through worship. In verses 4–6 it says that the one thing I want the most is the privilege of meditating in His temple, living in His presence every day of my life. The best way for me to do this is to praise Him and worship Him for everything He has done for me.

APPLICATION: Start your quiet time today worshipping God by singing Him a praise song. Then read Psalm 27. When finished, just sit completely still, wait for ten minutes, and let God minister to you.

WEEK 18—WEDNESDAY

Live Life to the Fullest

SCRIPTURE READING: John 10:7–11
THREE KEY PHRASES: The Mountains of Life—The Mundane Life—
The Maximum Life

I. The Mountains of Life

Just because we are Christians and have given our lives to Christ does not mean that we are going to be free from problems. Life is like a mountain; there is no easy path. You have to take it one step at a time. We will have mountains to climb with finances, health, family, business, and every area of our lives, but we have Christ with us to help us. He is like a ski lift to the top.

II. The Mundane Life

When we face mountains, we get discouraged, and life is just mundane. We get up at the same time, trudge off to work, come home, eat dinner, sit down, and watch television. This goes on day after day, with no excitement in our lives. Satan steals our joy, and life passes us by. This is not the way Christ intended our lives be.

III. The Maximum Life

God said in today's scriptures, "I have come to give you abundant life." Like a mountain climber reaching the peak, it is exciting and feels like He has a purpose. When we let Christ take us up our mountains and give all to Him, and when we finally get over the top, life will be exciting for us as well, because there is nothing like a mountaintop experience with God.

APPLICATION: If you are facing a mountain in your life today, ask God for strength to get over the top. He will guide you to the top if you will let Him. When you do, the fullness of life will return to you. Don't do it alone; go with God.

WEEK 18—THURSDAY
Speaking Truth to Unbelievers

SCRIPTURE READING: 2 Timothy 2:19–25
THREE KEY PHRASES: The Talk—The Trap—The Truth

I. The Talk
Many of us talk about Christ, what He means to us, and all the wonderful things He has done for us. We want others to have that experience as well. Therefore, we tell them about Christ, and sometimes they aren't going to believe us. We can't force our talk upon them. We must be an example of graciousness and kindness as we speak.

II. The Trap
Satan will trap us to lose our temper or be more forceful. When we speak too strongly and we turn people off, Satan has trapped their minds and hearts, and they will never believe.

III. The Truth
The Bible says, "You shall know the truth, and the truth shall set you free." We must spread truth, but as Paul said, to be effective we must be gentle and kind and let the Holy Spirit do the work. This is Christ's way.

APPLICATION: If you have the opportunity to witness to someone today, remember how to talk. Don't be forceful, but be gentle. Ask the Holy Spirit to speak through you and to convince their hearts. The rest is up to God, and He will bring in the harvest.

WEEK 18—FRIDAY

Joy-Stealers

SCRIPTURE READING: Philippians 1:1–11
THREE KEY WORDS: **Worry—Weariness—Willingness**

I. Worry

Sometimes as I go through life, I worry about certain things that I really need not worry about. Charles Swindoll says, "Worry is an inordinate anxiety about something that may or may not occur, and usually doesn't." Paul says, "Don't worry about anything, but in prayer and thanksgiving, turn it over to God."

II. Weariness

Weariness brings about stress. I get so stressed I get weary. Swindoll says stress is an intense strain over a situation we can't change or control. I can't control my job and future if I want to do God's will. He has to control it. This causes me stress which also brings fear into my life. Worry and weariness go hand-in-hand.

III. Willingness

I have to come to a point in my life where I just can let go and "let God." In my praise book today, it says I can commit my future and location, which causes me so much stress, to God and be willing to let God complete His work in me. If we do that, then we can have joy in our lives if we let God take control. Do it today.

APPLICATION: As you pray today, tell God that you are not going to worry about anything. You are casting all of your worries on Him to handle. Then be willing to follow whatever steps He wants you to take. This will help you from getting weary.

WEEK 19—MONDAY

Legalism

SCRIPTURE READING: Ephesians 4:1–11
THREE KEY PHRASES: The Slave of Legalism—The Sin of Legalism—
The Setting Free of Legalism

I. The Slave of Legalism
When we try to be religious by keeping the law, we are like slaves. We become a person of "dos and don'ts." We become slaves to good works. We really offend God if we become slaves to the law like the Pharisees.

II. The Sin of Legalism
When we are so dogmatic that we believe we are always right and try to push our beliefs on others, we are committing sin. In my early years of being a Christian, I did this all the time and offended others because it was religion without love. As a result, especially in your family, you can drive people away or, like with my children, cause bitterness.

III. The Setting Free of Legalism
Paul said that God sent Jesus to take the place of law and legalism. We are not under the law, but grace. We are God's children and have everything He has, and to show our love to others we must use law as guidelines, but not legalism. We are to love unconditionally.

APPLICATION: Don't become a "do and don't" person. Also, don't judge others. We are to leave that to God. Do as Jesus does by loving unconditionally. If you have been raised as a legalist Christian, ask God to set you free.

WEEK 19—TUESDAY

It Takes Just One

SCRIPTURE READING: Ephesians 4:17–32
THREE KEY PHRASES: One Man—One Mistake—One Mission

I. One Man

One person can cause HAVOC or HEAVEN. Historically, we have been influenced by one man many times. We have Hitler, Stalin, Saddam Hussein, and Osama Bin Laden as negative influences. These men each had an unfortunate effect on our world. On the positive side we have Abraham Lincoln, Winston Churchill, Franklin Roosevelt, and Ronald Reagan. They had a positive influence, but the one man who changed the world was Jesus Christ, and we have never been the same since.

II. One Mistake

As the scriptures say today, one man can bring great destruction in our lives, especially in our church. This is usually caused by gossip or angry feelings. I have seen it happen at our drug rehab center. One man is destroying our unity. We must not let Satan do that; we must be united.

III. One Mission

God appointed one man—His Son, Jesus Christ—to carry out His mission by dying for our sins so we can live forever with Him. Our mission, given to us in the book of Matthew, is to carry out Jesus's mission as well. It starts with one man—me—and a unified effort with like-minded people.

APPLICATION: If you have someone in your life who is causing you trouble, or problems in your church or ministry, go to that person and try to resolve it. Also ask God to give you a like spirit so you can help carry out His mission.

WEEK 19—WEDNESDAY

Miracles

SCRIPTURE READING: Exodus 15:19–27
THREE KEY PHRASES: God's Guidance—God's Graciousness—
God's Guidelines

I. **God's Guidance**

Like Moses, after a miracle takes place in our lives it is time to move on. But we often times face other battles or decisions. That is why I need God's guidance. Right now I am asking God to guide my decisions for the future. Please, Lord, guide me.

II. **God's Graciousness**

God is so good and gracious to us. We must not forget all the past miracles in our lives; His answers to prayer, His provisions for us, and His presence in our life daily. What a gracious God.

III. **God's Guidelines**

God has some guidelines that we must follow to find His will for our lives. Like today's scriptures, God had some conditions for commitment. We must listen to the voice of God through His Word, obey it, and do what is right. God will protect us and show us His purpose for our lives. Please Lord, help us do it today.

APPLICATION: If we want to know God's will for our lives, we must follow some guidelines, like loving Him with all of our hearts and souls, and loving our neighbor as ourselves. There is an old saying about trying to find God's will for your life. "When in doubt, don't." Satan is the author of confusion; God is the author of perfect peace.

WEEK 19—THURSDAY

Is *Work* Your God?

SCRIPTURE READING: Ecclesiastes 2:17–26
THREE KEY PHRASES: Our Identity—Our Influence—Our Inheritance

I. Our Identity
In today's busy world, some people try to find their identity in work. It is a status symbol. I try to impress others by telling them how hard I work. I brag about results, because it makes me feel important and accepted by these people. Solomon said it is all vanity, like chasing the wind.

II. Our Influence
We may influence a lot of people, and even impress them with our work, but God says this is an idol. We cannot put it before Him and expect to be blessed. God says our influence on others should be how we live for Him. Our daily work should influence and impact others.

III. Our Inheritance
Solomon says, "Why should we work so hard just to leave our inheritance to others?" It is foolish. We already have our inheritance in heaven. We are joint heirs with Christ. That is why we should influence others for heaven, so they will have an inheritance that will last forever.

APPLICATION: I heard it said that Satan was asked, "What is the best way to attack the Christian?" His reply was, "I will make them so busy in the world that they won't have time for God. A workaholic can be as bad as an alcoholic." God says to put Him first in everything we do, and this applies especially to work. Remember, even God rested one full day, and He is busier than all of us.

WEEK 19—FRIDAY

Eagle Flight

SCRIPTURE READING: Isaiah 40:27–31
THREE KEY PHRASES: Our Stress—Our Strength—Our Savior

I. Our Stress

As we go out each day and face the world, there is a lot of stress and strain. Because the way the world is today, we live in a pressure cooker. Like the scripture says, today we get weary, tired, discouraged, and sometimes we think we aren't going to make it. Many mornings when I get up, I feel that way.

II. Our Strength

Psalm 84:5 says, "Blessed is the man whose strength is in you." Proverbs 3:5–6 says, "Trust in the Lord with all your heart and lean not to your own understanding. In all your ways, acknowledge Him and He will direct your path." "Wait on the Lord and He will give you strength. We shall mount up like the eagles. We shall run and not be weary, we shall walk and not faint." We have to realize that we can't do it alone. We can only live today with God's strength.

III. Our Savior

We must realize that Jesus and the Holy Spirit live in our hearts, and we need to tap into their power daily. Let them guide, lead, and love us. We just need to put our total trust in Him and let Him ease our stress and give us strength. Do it today and every day.

APPLICATION: As you start your workday, pray to God and simply say, "Lord, I trust you with everything I do today. I understand that you are far better than I am at what I do, so today, Lord, I am leaning on you to do the best we can together." It will make your day much easier.

WEEK 20—MONDAY

Yes or No

SCRIPTURE READING: John 5:24–30
THREE KEY PHRASES: Yearn for Christ—Yes to Christ—Yield to Christ

I. **Yearn for Christ**
   As the scripture says, today many of us yearn for Christ; we study the scriptures and look for peace, joy, guidance, direction, and salvation. But salvation doesn't come by just yearning for Christ. He wants more.

II. **Yes to Christ**
   In order to have a relationship with Christ, the Son of God, we must say "yes" to Him. We must accept Him as our personal Lord and Savior so we can build a personal relationship with Him. We must say "yes" that we believe He died for our sins and rose again. Then we must ask for forgiveness for those sins. This is the real thing.

III. **Yield to Christ**
   Now that we have said "yes" to Christ, we must yield every part of our lives to Him. We must trust Him completely with our lives, entrust ourselves to the church, and serve Him daily. We must not only know the facts, we need to know the Savior. Yield today.

APPLICATION: If you have a yearning to know Christ, ask Him to come into your heart and be your Lord and Savior. Say "yes" to Him today. If you have already done so, yield everything you have to Him, and He will yearn to have fellowship with you. There is nothing better than being in the presence of God all day long.

WEEK 20—TUESDAY

Life and Death Matters

SCRIPTURE READING: Romans 8:12–18
THREE KEY PHRASES: The Lie—The Lion—The Lord

I. The Lie
Satan is the biggest liar on earth. He tries to make everything in the world look good to us so we will yield to the flesh—our ambitions, our desires, and our wants. The flesh tells us daily, "Eat, drink, and be merry." It is a lie.

II. The Lion
Just as in the jungle animals must survive by killing their prey, nature is violent. Something must die in the jungle so something else can live. The same is true spiritually. Satan roars like a lion to see whom he can devour. Interests of the flesh must succumb to interest of the spirit or else the interest of the spirit will succumb to the interest of the flesh. In the jungle of our heart, something must die so that something else can live. That something is our old nature when we give our life to Christ.

III. The Lord
We need the Lord's help to daily die in the flesh. It is a constant battle. As we go into the jungle every day we must say, "Lord, I yield my spirit and flesh today." Help me to survive in the jungle. Help me walk in the spirit today, I pray, and not be Satan's prey.

APPLICATION: As you start your day in prayer, ask God to put a hedge of protection around you from the evil one. Then do as the scripture says, "draw nigh unto God and He will draw nigh unto you. Cherish His promise that greater is He who is in you than He who is in the world."

WEEK 20—WEDNESDAY
So Many Blessings

SCRIPTURE READING: Ephesians 1:1–14
THREE KEY PHRASES: Our Burden—Our Bearer—Our Blessings

I. Our Burden
We all have personal disasters in life, and as a result, we carry heavy burdens. It could be the loss of a loved one, a financial disaster, a health problem, our future, or our children. These burdens can wear us down.

II. Our Bearer
God sent Jesus to die for us. After the resurrection, He sent the Holy Spirit to comfort us and help us to carry those burdens. In today's scripture it says that His presence in us is God's guarantee that He will give us what He has promised. His seal upon us is His guarantee that He will someday bring us to Himself.

III. Our Blessings
In today's scripture it says that because what Christ did for us, we have become gifts to God that He delights in. What a blessing that we are a gift to God. We are also a part of His family. We have forgiveness of sins; we are joint heirs with Christ. We have so many blessings that should overshadow our burdens. We should praise God daily for these blessings.

APPLICATION: The Bible says, "cast all of your burdens on Him because He cares for you." There is an old saying we are God's gift to us, and what we do is our gift back to God. Therefore, be a blessing to God by giving Him all of your burdens to bear for you. That is His job, not ours.

WEEK 20—THURSDAY

God's Help

SCRIPTURE READING: Luke 6:27–35
THREE KEY PHRASES: Lord Help Me—Lord Hear Me—Lord Heal Me

I. Lord Help Me
Today, Lord, I am tired and weary, trying to be obedient sometimes wears me down, and I think, "What's the use?" I really want to quit. Lord, help me not to quit today. Please help me. Please help me to be obedient to you today. Give me the strength I need. If we need help, that is exactly what God wants us to do.

II. Lord Hear Me
Lord, as I cry out to you today, please hear my cry. Be attentive to my every need. Lord, I know you hear my prayers. Help me to take the time to listen and hear you. Lord, I know it is hard to be obedient, but hear me when I say, fill me with your Spirit and help me walk in your Spirit today.

III. Lord Heal Me
Lord, my body is tired and aches. My spirit is weak. My emotions are wrought. I am tired and depressed. I see no hope for the future. Please touch and heal my body, soul, and spirit today. Lord, I need you today in a real way—*help me, hear me, heal me*. Thank you, Lord.

APPLICATION: I put this in the first person because many days I feel like everyone else. When I do, I just remember these three simple phrases, and God answers all three. What a privilege we have to cry out to our Father and have Him help us, hear us, and heal us. Praise Him for doing so.

WEEK 20—FRIDAY
Effective Prayer

SCRIPTURE READING: 1 John 3:21–24
THREE KEY PHRASES: Our Conscience—Our Condition—Our Confidence

I. Our Conscience
To have an effective prayer life, our conscience must be clear. We must not have any guilt about our sins; we must not have any doubts about our faith and our Christian walk. Our conscience must be crystal clear that everything is right with God.

II. Our Condition
Matthew 7:7–8 says we will receive from God what we ask of Him, but there are conditions. First, in today's scripture, we must obey God and do what pleases Him. That means believing in Jesus and also loving others. This also produces the clear conscience we need to be obedient.

III. Our Confidence
In today's scripture it says that if we follow the conditions and have a clear conscience, we can come to God with perfect assurance. We can trust and get whatever we ask for, because we are obeying Him and doing what pleases Him. To be effective, have a clear conscience, obey God's conditions, and be confident that He will answer.

APPLICATION: If you need to clear your conscience, ask God to forgive your sins. He will clear your heart and clear your mind. Then go forth with confidence and perfect assurance that He will hear and answer your prayer. That is how we are effective.

WEEK 21—MONDAY

Good News or Bad

SCRIPTURE READING: Luke 12:35–40
THREE KEY PHRASES: The Lord is Coming Soon—The Lord is Coming Suddenly—The Lord is Coming for Sure

I. **The Lord is Coming Soon**
As we look at all the things happening in today's world, they show that the Lord is coming soon. Everything points to the end times, and He will be here soon. If you study prophecy and the events leading up to His return, God is going to send Jesus back to earth to gather His family.

II. **The Lord is Coming Suddenly**
At the blink of an eye, the Lord will come. There will be no forewarning. The Bible says, "As a thief comes in the night, so shall the coming of the Lord be." We must all be waiting and watching. We all look forward to events taking place in our lives, but the greatest event to look forward to is the coming of our Lord and Savior.

III. **The Lord is Coming for Sure**
There is no getting away from it. The Bible says that someday *soon* and *sudden* the Lord's coming is *sure*. For some, that is good news. They are waiting and watching faithfully. For others, that is bad because they have never accepted Christ, and at the Lord's coming, they shall be left behind to suffer through seven years of trials and tribulations. We must be ready, but we must get others ready as well.

APPLICATION: As you meditate on the *soon*, *sudden*, and *sure* coming of the Lord, ask yourself a few questions. First, am I ready? Have I accepted Christ as my Savior, and is He in my heart? If He should come today, is there anything in my life that I would be ashamed of at His presence? If so, confess it to the Lord. The last question is, do I know someone in my family or do I have a friend at work who is not ready? If you answer yes to that question, then be committed to get those people ready by telling them about Jesus Christ. Do it now.

WEEK 21—TUESDAY

Dealing with Self-Doubt

SCRIPTURE READING: Psalm 26
THREE KEY WORDS: Sin—Sincerity—Safety

I. Sin

Sometimes when we commit sin, we have a guilty conscience and have self-doubt. I have become so used to being around sinful people that I get concerned about my salvation and my love for the Lord and my integrity for Him. Satan is the author of confusion, and if I am doing my best to live for God and to overcome sin, I should not doubt, because God is the author of perfect peace.

II. Sincerity

We must check my motives constantly and make sure we are sincere and are not doing things for the Lord just to please ourselves, but to please Him. Integrity and character come from sincerity. Lord, help us to be sincere for you and to love you more than anything in the world. Help us to not be insincere.

III. Safety

When we sin and doubt God, we have the safety of His promise that "these things I write that ye may know you have eternal life." *Don't doubt—depend on Him*—and He will *deliver you*. Please, Lord, help us daily to not doubt but to be sincere and trust you completely.

APPLICATION: The Bible says that "greater is He who is in you than he who is in the world." When Satan causes you to doubt, exercise your power and tell him, "Get behind thee, Satan," then read John 10:27–30. This will show that you are secure in Christ.

WEEK 21—WEDNESDAY

Change

SCRIPTURE READING: Acts 22:1–16
THREE KEY WORDS: Creation—Complaints—Comfort

I. Creation
When we think of creations, we only think of all of the physical things—the beauty of the environment, trees, sunsets, and people. But God also created emotions, feelings, and also change. I am a proof of change as I write this. God changes people dramatically, but in this high-tech world, things are changing faster than we are.

II. Complaints
As I go through changes, I complain a lot. I don't like getting older, I don't like the computer-driven world, I don't like the changes in our traditions in the church, the music, and dress codes. As I examine myself, I constantly complain about change. Accepting change is an attitude, and we have a choice. Therefore, I need to change my attitude about change and go with the flow.

III. Comfort
To help us accept change, God sometimes asks us to step outside of our comfort zone. We need to change things to reach people for Christ. As the old saying goes, "We sometimes have to change the method, but not the message." We need to ask God to help us, but out of all of this, there is one thing that will never *change*. That is God's Word and God's promises. He is the same yesterday, today, and forever. That gives me peace.

APPLICATION: Realize today that things are going to change whether we like it or not. As you pray, ask God to change your heart about change. Ask Him to help you to have an open mind in how our *methods, music,* and *ministry* can be used to reach more people for Christ. Then accept it and be part of that changing process.

WEEK 21—THURSDAY

Building Others

SCRIPTURE READING: Philippians 2:19–30
THREE KEY PHRASES: Affirming Others—Attention to Others—Allegiance to Others

I. Affirming Others

One of the things we need to do in our Christian life is affirming others by building them up and not putting them down. We live in a put-down world, and it really hurts people. As we talk to others today, ask God to help you to affirm them and say something good about them.

II. Attention to Others

One of the things I need to work on daily is my attention to others, especially my wife. She needs and deserves a lot of affirming and attention from me. I need to set aside my busy schedule, my self-indulgence in what I want to do, and give my attention to her. I also need to be attentive to the needs of others.

III. Allegiance to Others

Another important factor about building up people is to be loyal to them no matter what, just as Timothy was to Paul. No matter what happens, we should never let Satan destroy our allegiance to our fellow brothers and sisters in Christ.

APPLICATION: As you go about your activities today and come in contact with others, give someone a sincere compliment to affirm that person. If someone needs a listening ear, give your attention by listening to what that person has to say. Also, if someone needs to be reaffirmed that you love that person, make sure you do so. Be a builder today.

WEEK 21—FRIDAY

What Will Happen

SCRIPTURE READING: 2 Timothy 4:1–8
THREE KEY PHRASES: The Certainty of Death—The Crowning of Death—The Celebration of Death

I. **The Certainty of Death**
We don't like talking about death, but it is a fact that someday we are all going to check out of here and spend eternity either in heaven or hell. That is as certain as death itself. The question is where will you spend eternity?

II. **The Crowning of Death**
In today's scripture, Paul says that if we are saved, and working and living for God, He has a crown of righteousness waiting for us in heaven. We must do our best for Him so we will have a crown fit for a king when we see Him.

III. **The Celebration of Death**
It is hard to think of death as a celebration because we'll be leaving our loved ones, but for the Christian, it is a celebration. We pass from death to life with Jesus. Our everlasting life will be so glorious we cannot begin to describe it. Be ready to celebrate Jesus for all eternity.

APPLICATION: As we start our day, we should live it to the fullest as if it were our last day on earth, because it could be. Be *certain* you are ready for that *crowning* day in heaven when the *celebration* will be forever. Pray for God to show you others who need to be certain as well.

WEEK 22—MONDAY
Satisfaction

SCRIPTURE READING: Ecclesiastes 2
THREE KEY PHRASES: Self Satisfaction—Satan's Satisfaction—Savior's Satisfaction

I. Self Satisfaction
In today's world we try everything to please self—big houses, big cars, our careers, material possessions, hobbies, and changing our appearance. It is all about "me" and having fun, but in today's scripture Solomon said he tried that. He had anything he wanted—fame, money, politics, great business—but nothing satisfied him.

II. Satan's Satisfaction
If self doesn't satisfy, then like Solomon, we turn to Satan—deceit, wine, women, and song. Let's just have a little fun with lust, sex, going to clubs, music, drugs, a mistress, and an affair. All of these things sound good, but Solomon had all of these and still wasn't satisfied.

III. Savior's Satisfaction
As Solomon said, "When you add it all up, it is all foolishness." He said it is like chasing the wind. There is only one thing that satisfies and that is fearing God, loving God, and putting Him first in everything we do. Serve God and be holy as He is holy. As Solomon also said, "Fearing God is the beginning of wisdom." Be wise today and follow Him.

APPLICATION: If you are running the rat race of life, searching for self-satisfaction, be careful. Burnout will lead you into Satan's deceit. Ask the Savior to take control of your life. Surrender everything to Him, because as the old hymn says, only Jesus will satisfy our souls. Only He can take our heart and make us whole.

WEEK 22—TUESDAY

God is My Boss

SCRIPTURE READING: Colossians 3: 22–25
THREE KEY PHRASES: Witnessing at Work—Willingness at Work—Wonderfulness at Work

I. **Witnessing at Work**
As today's scripture says, we should be a good witness at work. We should use our job as a pulpit to witness to others. They should see a difference in us. We should do our job daily, not only for our boss, but do the best for our Father in heaven, who is our "Big Boss."

II. **Willingness at Work**
Part of that witnessing is to be willing to go the extra mile. Whatever the boss asks, we should do as long as we don't compromise our standards. We should be willing to do so. This willingness will be a strong example to others. As a great coach once said, "First I will be my best, then I will be first."

III. **Wonderfulness at Work**
Part of this witnessing will be having a good attitude about what we do. We should feel like our job is wonderful, that we have the best job available, and we are happy and content. Your attitude will show your witness for Christ. Many times it is our attitude and not our aptitude that will determine our altitude in life, especially at work. Give it your best shot each day.

APPLICATION: Ask God to help you to be a witness at work by leading by example. Be willing to do whatever it takes and make your work a wonderful place for you and others, with a good attitude as your witness.

WEEK 22—WEDNESDAY

People Are Watching

SCRIPTURE READING: Deuteronomy 6:1–9
THREE KEY PHRASES: Our Earthly Example—Our Educational Example—Our Eternal Example

I. Our Earthly Example
The scripture says today that we are to be an example to our children and grandchildren as we walk the earth. Every day we are to be a Christ-like example, loving and caring for others. We are not under the law, but should use the law as our guidelines to be an example to others.

II. Our Educational Example
Today's scripture says that we are to teach our loved ones constantly about God and His Word. When we sit, when we walk, when we lie down, when we rise up, we are always to be teaching, but the best lesson we can teach is by the example we set on a daily basis.

III. Our Eternal Example
God became flesh for us and walked among us to give us our example for eternity. In everything Jesus did, He was obeying the Father's will. When He preached, healed, and even when He washed the disciples' feet, He was setting an example for us. He wanted this so much for us that He died for us, so we could spend eternity with Him. Thank you, Jesus, for your example.

APPLICATION: There is an old saying that says, "Lead by example, judge by results." Throughout the day, ask God to help you be a good example to others. Teach your loved ones as well, so we all can enjoy eternal benefits. It can only be done with God's help, one day at a time.

WEEK 22—THURSDAY

Prayer

SCRIPTURE READING: Luke 11:5–11
THREE KEY WORDS: Persistence—Petitions—Praise

I. Persistence

In today's scripture, Jesus uses a great example of persistence. We are to keep asking, keep seeking, and keep knocking. God will always hear, receive, and answer us. It might not be on our time schedule or the answer we are looking for, but He will answer. It is the same persistence we use to make it through another day, every day.

II. Petitions

God also wants us to be specific in our request. Make your petitions known to Him. There is nothing too big or nothing too small for God. Every petition we make is important to Him, and He personally handles every petition we send to Him.

III. Praise

Part of our prayer time should be spent praising God for what He has already done for us and what He is going to do for us. Our faith must be strong, and we should praise Him and adore Him in prayer and worship time. Praise God from whom all blessing flow. Be persistent, tell Him your petitions, and praise Him for the answers.

APPLICATION: If you have been praying for a certain petition for a long time and you are about to give up, be persistent and keep asking, seeking, and knocking. Know that God is hearing you. Pray in faith and then praise Him when He answers, no matter what the answer may be.

WEEK 22—FRIDAY

Thinking

SCRIPTURE READING: Philippians 4:1–9
THREE KEY PHRASES: Guard Your Thinking—Guard Your Talking—Guard Your Testimony

I. Guard Your Thinking
Zig Ziglar once said, "You are what you are and where you are because of what gets into your mind. You change what you are and where you are by changing what goes into your mind." The Bible says, "Guard your affections, because they affect everything you do." Sometimes I have let my guard down, and as a result, my thinking has caused me to be miserable. I must put a guard around my mind and eyes so I can keep my thinking right.

II. Guard Your Talking
We also have a bad habit of talking about the pleasures of the world and not the pleasures of God, such as off-color jokes or stories, gossip, and exaggerations. These things don't please God. James says, "The tongue is the hardest thing to control." Our thinking affects our talking. This is why we need to guard both.

III. Guard Your Testimony
Our *thinking* and *talking* will affect our *testimony* to others. This is why Paul gives us a list in today's scriptures that we should think about so we can be a good testimony. Be a *good thinker*, a *good talker*, and you will be a good *testimony*.

APPLICATION: As you pray today, ask God to put a hedge of protection around your thought life to keep the enemy from entering. Also ask Him to take control of your tongue and not to say bad things about others. Ask Him to help you be a good testimony today as well.

WEEK 23—MONDAY

Life

SCRIPTURE READING: Psalm 32
THREE KEY PHRASES: The Experiments of Life—The Examples of Life—The Enjoyments of Life

I. The Experiments of Life

As we start through life and as we get a little older, we will experiment with different things, some good, some bad. These experiments can lead us to happiness or destruction. It may start with a first cigarette at an early age, then alcohol, then drugs, then illicit sex, and before we know it, our life is destroyed and on the trash pile. God says we don't need to experiment with Him, just give our lives to Him.

II. The Examples of Life

There are many examples in the Bible and in life when these experiments went from *destruction* to *delightfulness*. I am also one of these examples, and if we look at a lot of famous people, we will find many examples as well from all walks of life, such as business, sports, and politics. For instance, Moses murdered a person, David committed adultery and had Bathsheba's husband killed, Abraham lied about Sarah, Peter denied Christ three times, and Paul murdered Christians before he came to Christ, but God used all of these people greatly in the Bible.

III. The Enjoyments of Life

We think enjoyment comes from sin and that sin is fun, but the bottom line is that the only true enjoyment comes from walking in the fruits of the Spirit and having the love and enjoyment of Christ. As the old saying goes, "Christ is the answer, the only answer."

APPLICATION: Make a commitment that you are not going to experiment with anything that could lead to trouble. If you have children, find out if they are experimenting with anything themselves. God is full of grace and mercy and will forgive us if we fail, but the consequences to others can be devastating. Enjoy your day by walking in the fruits of the Holy Spirit.

WEEK 23—TUESDAY

Alpha and Omega

SCRIPTURE READING: Revelations 22:6–13
THREE KEY PHRASES: The Beginning—The Between—The Benediction

I. The Beginning
Jesus has been before the foundation of the world. As part of the Trinity, He was God and was with God. Also in the beginning was the Word. The Word was God, and the Word was with God. Our life has a beginning as well; we don't know how long it will last, and we all have a purpose while we are here.

II. The Between
There is a beginning and there is an end to life. In the between we are to do our best to live for Jesus. He is our example. We are to love others as we love ourselves, to mend broken hearts, to tell others the good news. It seems like a long time, but it goes by so fast.

III. The Benediction
Someday we will hear the bugle or the trumpet sound and that will mean the end, the benediction. There is a beginning and an end to everything. The most important thing, since we don't know when it will take place, is to be ready when the end comes, because there will be a new beginning that is absolutely unbelievable for those who are in Christ. If we do it right, it will be a blessing.

APPLICATION: It is never too late for a new beginning whether you are 10 or 110 years old. If you need to confess sin as it suggests in 1 John 1:9, do so today, or if you need to accept Christ as your Savior, do so today as well. "Behold, old things will pass away and all things will become new for you. Today is the first day of the rest of your life."

WEEK 23—WEDNESDAY

Be an Encouragement

SCRIPTURE READING: Romans 1:1–15
THREE KEY WORDS: Empathy—Encouragement—Example

I. Empathy

When people are going through tough times, we need to empathize with them and not sympathize with them. Sometimes we hurt people by saying, "I feel sorry for you." They don't want sympathy, they want empathy. In other words, put ourselves in their shoes and try to understand how they feel or why they are doing what they are doing.

II. Encouragement

I think one of the greatest gifts God has given me is to be an encourager. Today take time to write a note to or call someone who needs encouragement. It must be sincere and not flattery. You cannot give people too much encouragement. In fact, in a recent study, the thing people said they wanted most is appreciation, encouragement, and acceptance.

III. Example

When I am down, I need to be an example to others. I shouldn't feel sorry for myself. The best way for me to get out of the pit is to find someone else I can help to get out of the pit and call that person to offer encouragement. That way we will both be helped.

APPLICATION: Ask God to bring someone into your mind or life today who needs you to be an example with empathy and understanding, and also be encouraging to that person.

WEEK 23—THURSDAY

Lend an Ear

SCRIPTURE READING: 1 Corninthians 12
THREE KEY WORDS: Listening—Learning—Loving

I. Listening

As I have said many times, we listen to understand, not to reply. In my busy everyday world, I need to take time to listen, especially to my wife. Many people need to just talk to someone. They need a listening ear. Also, we need to take the time to listen to God and what He wants to say to us. Take time to listen.

II. Learning

By listening to others, we are also learning—about what is important to them, where they are hurting, what their needs are, and what we can do to help. By listening to God we are learning His Word and also His will for our lives. Take time to listen.

III. Loving

We are to care for one another by using the gifts God has given us. One of the best ways I can love my wife is to listen, and one of the ways I can learn to love God more is to listen for His still small voice. He shows His love to me by listening to what I need and meeting that need. Take time to listen to God and to others. This will enhance your relationship more than anything else.

APPLICATION: As you come in contact with people today, ask God to help you to not be a talker but a good listener. Tune into what they are saying and once you understand them, kneel and talk to God about their situation. Then time to listen and hear from Him.

WEEK 23—FRIDAY

Lightening the Load

SCRIPTURE READING: Philippians 4:10–20
THREE KEY WORDS: Concern—Caring—Contentment

I. Concern

As we go through the game of life, we should have concern for others. Some people are going through some real tough times and have a very heavy load to carry. They don't know how they are going to make it. If we know someone like that, we should be concerned for that person and help them lighten their load.

II. Caring

Not only should we be concerned for this person, but we should also care for him or her as well. In other words, what can we do to lighten the load? Does this person need a word of encouragement? Can we help financially or help with some physical need? Jesus was a caring person, and we need to be as well.

III. Contentment

When we are caring, that person will be more contented and so will we. When the load of life gets heavy, find someone else with a heavier load. Help lighten that person's load, and your load will become lighter. You will find contentment in helping others and also contentment in Christ.

APPLICATION: Think of a person you know at work or a family member or friend who is going through a rough time and is carrying a heavy load. Call that person today and make an appointment to get together so you can do whatever needs to be done to lighten their load. Help that person to cast all their cares on Jesus, because He cares more than anyone else.

WEEK 24—MONDAY

Cross and Crown

SCRIPTURE READING: John 3
THREE KEY PHRASES: The Condemned—The Cross—The Crown

I. The Condemned

For those who don't trust Christ, they are condemned to eternal death. We came into this world condemned as sinners; we all have sinned, and have come short of the Glory of God. Since the sin in the garden, we have been condemned as sinners. This is our state at birth, but doesn't have to be at death.

II. The Cross

God the Father provided a way for us to overcome our condemnation. He loved us so much that He sent His only begotten Son to the cross to die for us. Jesus did not come to condemn the world, but to save it from condemnation. There is no condemnation for those who trust Christ. We have eternal life.

III. The Crown

There are many crowns in life, but the only one that really matters is the crown that we get from the Father. There is a crown in heaven for me for the work I have done for Christ here on earth. This is the only promise I need to help me face each day.

APPLICATION: If you are personally suffering from feeling condemned, ask Christ to forgive you and let the peace that passes all understanding keep your heart and mind in Christ Jesus. Also, if you know someone who feels the same way, make a commitment to talk and pray with that person as soon as possible.

WEEK 24—TUESDAY

Testing and Trials

SCRIPTURE READING: Hebrews 11:32–40
THREE KEY PHRASES: God's Purpose in Testing—God's Participation in Testing—God's Promise of Testing

I. God's Purpose in Testing

Sometimes as we go through life we have great trials and tests. If we believe Romans 8:28, we know that these are for our good. We don't understand at the time, but later we do see that even though we didn't like it, we had to go through it. During these times we must really trust God.

II. God's Participation in Testing

Every person has a particular test that is different than ours. For some it is financial, health, wayward children, disease, divorce, or the death of a loved one. Although we have our personal tests, the purpose is all the same, and is to put our faith and trust in God.

III. God's Promise of Testing

We must take all of the promises in God's Word and believe that He will fulfill all His promises. It may not always be what we want, but like in Hebrews 11, some came through it, and God protected them. Others came through the test with as much faith but lost their lives during the test, but the purpose was that God knew it was better for them on the other side. Trust God completely while going through your test.

APPLICATION: If you are going through a real test right now in your life, ask God for special grace and mercy. Read Hebrews 11 completely. Study the lives of the people in the Hall of Faith in that chapter. Also remember the promises from God during your test. He says, "My grace is sufficient, and My mercy endures forever."

WEEK 24—WEDNESDAY
God is Everywhere

SCRIPTURE READING: Psalm 139
THREE KEY PHRASES: God's Pursuit—God's Protection—God's Presence

I. God's Pursuit
God loves us so much that He wants us to realize that He is there to meet our needs no matter what. No matter how tough it gets, He wants us to pursue Him so He can help and be with us because He loves us as one of His own.

II. God's Protection
God is our shelter, our refuge and fortress, and our hiding place in times of trouble. He is also our shepherd who guides day by day, our champion who helps us, and an inheritance who wants to satisfy our souls. God is everything.

III. God's Presence
In today's scripture, God is with us wherever we go. If we go to the den of sin, He is there. If we go to the church, He is there. At our work, He is there. God knows our every thought and plan. No matter where we go, God is with us, so we shouldn't go where God doesn't want to go. Let Him lead you, guide you, pursue you, and protect you. This is your only hope.

APPLICATION: In your prayer time today, tell God that you are so hungry and thirsty for His presence in your life that you are going to put forth an all out pursuit for His presence and protection in your life to be the person He wants you to be. Then go do it.

WEEK 24—THURSDAY
He Died for Me

SCRIPTURE READING: Isaiah 53
THREE KEY PHRASES: The Tree—The Task—The Triumph

I. The Tree
"Oh, can it be, upon a tree that my Savior died for me? My soul is thrilled, my heart is filled to think He died for me on the tree." Jesus could have saved Himself, but He chose to die for us personally so we wouldn't have to go to hell. He bore our punishment on that tree so that we might live.

II. The Task
Jesus knew from the day He was born that He would go to that tree. He knew that He would suffer and die on that tree. He carried out His task here on earth of teaching the gospel, healing, and performing miracles, while being ridiculed by friends and family. He never took His eye off of the task of the tree. That was His purpose in being here. Jesus's only mission in life was to do His Father's will, which included the old rugged cross.

III. The Triumph
Nails could not have kept Jesus on the cross if His love for us had not held Him there. The tree was only the beginning; the triumph came when He arose from the grave and came back to life again. Because of the *tree*, the *task*, and the *triumph* of the grave, I now have the *trophy* of eternal life with Him.

APPLICATION: As you pray today, meditate on the saying, "When I think of where He brought me from to where I am today, that is the reason why I love Him so." Also sing the first verse of the *Old Rugged Cross*, and then make a commitment to the task of telling others about the *tree* and the *triumph* so they can get their *trophy* as well.

WEEK 24—FRIDAY
Giving Away Happiness

SCRIPTURE READING: Proverbs 11:16–26
THREE KEY WORDS: Hope—Help—Happiness

I. Hope
There are no hopeless situations; we only lose hope in certain situations. Sometimes I feel hopeless, especially when I look at my future. There are so many people today who feel they have no hope whatsoever, especially the ones who have no family, are lonely, are in poor health, or are facing death. They feel hopeless.

II. Help
What we give more than what we get produces joy and happiness in our lives. If we want to remove that hopeless feeling, one of the best ways to do so is to help others with their hopelessness. We need to help others to be a little happier, and it will help us as well.

III. Happiness
In a *USA Today* article about happiness, it stated that some of the keys to happiness were strong marriages, family ties, and lasting friendships. Another important key to being happy was being spiritual and having a good self-image. If some of these are missing in our lives, the way to produce them is by doing the above things for others as well as ourselves. Start today.

APPLICATION: If you feel hopeless today, remember God says, "I will never leave you nor forsake you. I am always with you." Work hard to strengthen your marriage and friendships. Ask for help from others. Also remember that God said we are created in His image and that will build your self-image. To quote the late Ethel Waters, "God doesn't sponsor no flops."

WEEK 25—MONDAY

I Matter to God

SCRIPTURE READING: Luke 15:1–7
THREE KEY PHRASES: God's Sheep—God's Shelter—God's Sacrifice

I. God's Sheep
The Bible says that we are like sheep that have gone astray, but the shepherd loves His sheep and even knows them by name. God the shepherd knows His sheep as well. He knows the numbers of hairs on our heads. God loves us that much. We matter to Him.

II. God's Shelter
When I was saved, God took residence in my heart as the Holy Spirit. This is our safety net. It is possible for us to stray away, but God will always be there for us no matter how far we go. Never forget that God is our shelter in stormy times.

III. God's Sacrifice
God loved us so much that He sacrificed His only begotten Son as a lamb on the cross. When we were lost, He left the ninety-nine to bring us back to the shelter. Jesus is my good shepherd. He knows us and we know Him. He loves, guides, and protects us. What a wonderful savior.

APPLICATION: As believers in Christ, we sometimes kill our wounded by not working to bring them back into the fold. If you know someone who has strayed from Christ, be a good shepherd and do your best to bring that person home through prayer and reaching out to meet their needs. Each person matters that much to God.

WEEK 25—TUESDAY
The Gospel

SCRIPTURE READING: Galatians 1:1–10
THREE KEY PHRASES: The Source of the Gospel—The Scam of the Gospel—The Spreading of the Gospel

I. The Source of the Gospel

In Galatians, Paul tells the people that there is only one source for the gospel, and that source is Jesus Christ. There is no other gospel than the fact that Jesus is the Son of God. He died on the cross for our sins, arose on the third day, and is coming back again for us. We must accept Him as our Savior.

II. The Scam of the Gospel

As Paul also said in Galatians, there are people who scam with the gospel. They preach a false doctrine, or they are in it for the money. They scam people by preaching what they want to hear and also by playing on people's emotions. We must be on guard at all times. God's Word has never changed.

III. The Spreading of the Gospel

Paul says there are a lot of people who have never heard the gospel and also a great number who are hearing a false gospel. This is why Jesus gave us the great commission to spread the gospel and to make disciples so they will have a solid foundation.

APPLICATION: Realize that Jesus is the only source for the truth of the gospel. "Ye shall know the truth and the truth shall set you free." As you study the scriptures today, ask God to reveal truth to you and also take that truth to someone else. As you speak, tap into the source and spread the truth.

WEEK 25—WEDNESDAY

You Can Believe It

SCRIPTURE READING: Acts 1:1–11
THREE KEY PHRASES: The Death—The Doubt—The Decision

I. The Death

It is a fact that Jesus was born from the Virgin Mary and lived on earth for thirty-three years and that He was also the Son of God. He performed miracles and taught with the power to prove His authenticity. It is also a fact that He died on the cross for our sins and was buried in the tomb.

II. The Doubt

Many in that day did not believe that Jesus was who He said He was. Even yet, today many people doubt who He was, but there was also the declaration that He would arise from the grave on the third day to complete the prophecy of the death, burial, and resurrection. This is also a fact, as He was seen by more than 500 people, and today the Holy Spirit lives within us to prove it as well.

III. The Decision

With all that has been said and written, it is our decision as to whether we believe it or not. My decision is to accept and believe it so some day that I can spend eternity with Him. The price is just too high to not believe it by simple faith. I am not willing to gamble on that decision.

APPLICATION: It is a fact that death is certain, and there is no doubt about Jesus being who He said He was. Make a decision today that you are going to accept who He is once and for all, and that you are also going to tell this wonderful news to others. Now go do it.

WEEK 25—THURSDAY
Always on Call

SCRIPTURE READING: Psalm 34
THREE KEY PHRASES: God's Call—God's Cry—God's Children

I. God's Call
When we are discouraged, depressed, need someone to talk to, are sick and need healing, need financial help, or our children are astray, God is always on call. We might not be able to get in touch with someone else, but we can always get in touch with God. Call on Him today.

II. God's Cry
We not only need to cry out to God for help, but today's scriptures say that when we cry out to Him, He will answer us and will free us from all our fears. We need to cry out to God to free us today.

III. God's Children
As God's children, we need to revere Him; for when we do this, our Father will supply our needs. He says we will never lack any good thing. His eyes are always intently watching His children. He gives attention when we call and cry out to Him. What a loving father.

APPLICATION: If you are discouraged or depressed today, call out to God. He will hear your cry, and He will take away your fear. As His child, give reverence to Him today so He can supply whatever need you have this very moment. Remember, His eyes see your every need, and His ears hear your every call. Let Him be your loving Father today.

WEEK 25—FRIDAY
The Cross

SCRIPTURE READING: Ephesians 2:14–18
THREE KEY PHRASES: Glimpse of the Cross—Grateful for the Cross—
The Grace from the Cross

I. **Glimpse of the Cross**
As we go through our busy schedules each day, we need to take time to not only glimpse the cross, but to focus on the cross. We have a cross by our house on a mountainside that lights up every night. This reminds me of what God did for me when He sent Jesus to the cross.

II. **Grateful for the Cross**
All of us should be so grateful that Christ died for us so we would be reunited with God and not have to spend eternity in hell. The cross was meant for me, but Jesus took my place. He also took your place. What an awesome act of love. Be grateful today.

III. **The Grace from the Cross**
As it says in the scripture today, God did this to cancel the whole system of the Law so we could all be saved by grace. I am so grateful that I don't have to work my way to heaven. Take a glimpse and be grateful for God's grace today.

APPLICATION: As you pray today, thank God that you don't have to work your way to heaven. Take time to meditate and glimpse the cross. Be grateful for all God has done for you and spend time praising Him for His wonderful grace and mercy. Sing your favorite hymn to Him right now.

WEEK 26—MONDAY

Extreme Makeover

SCRIPTURE READING: Ephesians 1:3–14
THREE KEY WORDS: Accepted—Awesome—Arrived

I. Accepted or Special

There is a very popular television show today called "Extreme Makeover." Last year 15 million cosmetic procedures were performed. Women represented 80 percent of these procedures and 20 percent were by men, but the number of men is on the rise. They spend thousands of dollars and go through extreme physical pain for these procedures. They don't realize that transformation takes place from the inside out. No matter how much they change the outside, it won't change them on the inside. In verses 4 and 5 it says that we are chosen by God personally to be accepted into His family. We are accepted by Him the way we are which makes us special.

II. Awesome or Significant

People have these procedures because it seems like an awesome thing to do and it makes them significant. In verse 7 it says that we were not only chosen by God, but we are redeemed through His blood for the forgiveness of sins to be His children. That is the highest price ever paid for you. Therefore, in God's eyes you are an awesome and significant person. That should build your self-image more than anything else.

III. Arrived or Secure

When people have these extreme makeovers, they feel they have arrived, but how disappointed they are later. In verses 13 and 14, God says He seals you with the Holy Spirit and we will receive our inheritance when we get to Heaven. No matter what, we are accepted, we are secure, and nobody can ever break that seal. What security we have in Him.

APPLICATION: As you pray today, I simply want you to meditate on the high price God paid by giving His own Son to die for you. Meditate also on how special, significant and secure you really are in His sight. How awesome is that!

WEEK 26—TUESDAY

Praying with Boldness

SCRIPTURE READING: Psalms 6
THREE KEY PHRASES: Your Approach—Your Appreciation—Your Answer

I. Your Approach

When we pray to our Father, He wants us to be bold and open. Don't be apprehensive about telling it like it is. Look at David in today's scripture. He said, "I am weak, so pity me. I am upset and disturbed with life. I am gloomy. I am worn out with pain. Heal me." David was upset with life, and he let God know it.

II. Your Appreciation

When we go to the Father, we should pour out all of our appreciation for His blessings to us. We should praise Him for what He has done for us. We should be so thankful for our families, our health, and material blessings. God wants to hear that as well.

III. Your Answer

In Psalms 6:9, David claims victory over all of His enemies by saying, "The Lord has heard me, and He will answer all of my prayers." We must wait and be patient. Sometimes the answer might be no and a lot of times yes, but He will always answer. This is a great promise.

APPLICATION: As you approach God before the throne of grace today, pour out your heart to Him. If you are angry, tell Him so. If you are hurting, feel lonely, sick, or under pressure, be truthful with God and let it all hang out. The Bible says His understanding is unlimited, so He will understand. He will also lift you up. That is a promise from our Father who loves us.

WEEK 26—WEDNESDAY
Yielding Control

SCRIPTURE READING: Romans 8:1–11
THREE KEY WORDS: Separate—Surrender—Security

I. Separate
If we are going to find peace and joy in life, we must separate from the world and our worldly desires. If we follow the ways of the world and our sinful nature, we can't ever please God.

II. Surrender
If we are going to overcome the desire of the flesh, we must surrender ourselves completely to the power of the Holy Spirit. This is the way we please God. It also leads to life and peace. Following after the world leads to death, so if we follow our sinful nature, we will die and won't please God. If we follow the Holy Spirit, we will live and find peace. This is reason enough to surrender.

III. Security
When we surrender everything to the Holy Spirit, we have the security that the same power that raised Jesus from the dead will do the same for us. We will be raised to heaven, but we also have the same power while we live here on earth. That is what true security is all about.

APPLICATION: As you go into the world today, go as a witness for Christ, but also remember that we are never to compromise our convictions for doing so. We must separate ourselves from the world so they won't bring us down. Before you go, just surrender yourself to the Holy Spirit and ask Him to use you. Then go with the security that He is with you all the way.

WEEK 26—THURSDAY

God Can Save Anyone

SCRIPTURE READING: 1 Timothy 2
THREE KEY WORDS: Authority—Answer—Anyone

I. Authority

God tells us to pray for our leaders who have authority over us, such as our boss, teacher, and government leaders. But God also says to pray for everyone that has authority, no matter how bad they are. Paul was a cruel and wicked man, and said "I am the worst of sinners," but God saved him and used him greatly.

II. Answer

The answer to the wickedness of any person—leader, worker, spouse, child—is Christ. He came into the world so that whosoever calls upon the name of the Lord shall be saved, no matter who it is. There are no degrees of sin with God. God sent Christ to reconcile this world to Him.

III. Anyone

As I said a moment ago, this is for everyone. It seems horrible that Saddam Hussein, Osama Bin Laden, or people so wicked could be saved if they accepted Christ. Paul was like this before he was saved. Anyone can call upon Christ and be saved, and like Paul, they can be greatly changed. Pray for anyone and everyone, no matter how bad they are.

APPLICATION: We must remember that it is biblical for us to be under the authority of our government, whether we like it or not. But it is also our responsibility to pray for our leaders. No one person is too bad for God to save. It is hard, but as a Christian, we are to pray for everybody, good and bad alike.

WEEK 26—FRIDAY
Three Crosses

SCRIPTURE READING: Luke 23:32–49
THREE KEY PHRASES: The Sinner—The Saint—The Savior

I. The Sinner
On the three crosses were Christ and two others. One of them refused to accept Christ. He was a sinner just like me, but he mocked Jesus and did not believe Jesus was the Christ. He was dying in sin. All have sinned and come short of the glory of God. Unfortunately, when they die in sin, they go to an eternal hell.

II. The Saint
On the other cross was a man dying in sin. He recognized that he was a sinner and that Jesus was the Son of God, and right then and there, he accepted Jesus Christ as his Lord and Savior, which proves that you can get saved anywhere at any time. You can go immediately from sinner to saint. Christ is always available, but you should not run the risk of waiting until the last minute.

III. The Savior
On the middle cross was a man dying for sin. He could die for me and others because He was the only begotten Son of God. The center cross made all the difference in the world. We can either die to an eternal heaven or eternal hell. The choice is ours.

APPLICATION: When we came into the world, we were the same as the men on the crosses next to Christ. We were born in sin and deserved nothing from God, but because of the center cross, we can be born again and spend eternity in heaven with Him who was on that center cross. We must go tell that message to others every day. Start today.

WEEK 27—MONDAY

Trust God

SCRIPTURE READING: Luke 4:14–22
THREE KEY PHRASES: The Nature of God—The Need for God—The Necessity of God

I. The Nature of God

Sometimes when things get tough in life, we try to figure everything out. What is the purpose for God letting this happen? Why is He allowing this to come into my life? What does God have in mind for me or am I being punished for something? We try to figure out God's nature, and we cannot.

II. The Need for God

God knew we would try to do this, and that is why He sent Jesus. We can't figure it out. All things work together for God. We are to trust and obey Him. Jesus came to meet every need we have—spiritual, physical, mental, and financial. He came to set us free from sin and to save our souls.

III. The Necessity for God

God is necessary in our lives through Jesus Christ. Obeying Him should be our highest goal. This is the only path to happiness and joy in our lives. The only hope we have for now and eternity is Jesus Christ. Lord, help me today, I pray.

APPLICATION: When we accepted Christ as our Savior, our old nature died and our new nature in Christ came alive. However, we still need to ask God to help us live for Him daily. That is a necessity for our everyday life. Ask God to help you to walk in that new nature today and every day.

WEEK 27—TUESDAY

Live Accordingly

SCRIPTURE READING: Colossians 1:15–18
THREE KEY WORDS: Ethics—Embarrassment—Eternity

I. Ethics
As you read the scripture and the devotion, you'll notice there are a lot of people who don't practice what they preach. We know what we should do, and we even say the right things, but do we really live that way? To not do so is unethical and someday it will come back to haunt you. What goes around comes around.

II. Embarrassment
When you violate ethics and it catches up with you, it is a real embarrassment. It will destroy your integrity, embarrass your family, damage your reputation, ruin relationships, and follow you for life. Think of people who were leaders in sports, business, politics, and even ministry. When they were caught doing unethical things, their reputations were tarnished.

III. Eternity
When we die, we have a promise from God that we will spend eternity with Him, but what will we be remembered for? Our legacy is measured by *faith—family—friendships*. What will you leave behind?

APPLICATION: No matter what comes your way today, when making decisions, be sure to ask yourself, "What would Jesus do?" Jesus is our ethical role model. Never compromise your ethics and you will avoid embarrassment.

WEEK 27—WEDNESDAY

Lusters in Life

SCRIPTURE READING: Psalm 119:1–6
THREE KEY PHRASES: Learning God's Word—The Light in God's Word—The Life in God's Word

I. Learning God's Word

There is an old saying, "To know the author of the Bible, read His books." We can learn daily from reading God's Word. We can stay pure by reading God's Word. We can find His will for our life. Every time we open the Book, we should say, God help me to learn something today.

II. The Light in God's Word

The Bible says, "Happy are those who obey God's Word. Happy are those who look for God's will. Happy is the person who meditates day and night in God's Word." The light of life is not found in Las Vegas or Hollywood; the light of life is found in God's Word.

III. The Life in God's Word

There is real life and power in God's Word. It will keep us from sin. It will show us what to do. If we open our eyes, we will see wonderful things in God's Word. The lifeline to life is God's Word and the power of the Holy Spirit is His Word. Just as food sustains physical life, God's Word is food for our spiritual life. Read it daily.

APPLICATION: As you read God's Word today, look for a key verse that speaks to you. Write it down and then ask God for the willpower to memorize it.

WEEK 27—THURSDAY

Prayer

SCRIPTURE READING: Ephesians 3:14–21
THREE KEY PHRASES: Prayer Worrier—Prayer Warrior—Prayer Winners

I. **Prayer Worrier**
When we pray, many times all we do is pour out our worries and problems to God. We unload about things we are worrying about—finances, family matters, health, or relationships. But prayer should be more than just problem-solving. It should also be a time for praise and worship.

II. **Prayer Warrior**
Prayer is not an easy thing. It takes time, effort, and commitment on our part. We also have to discipline our minds and hearts in prayer so we don't wander. We have to stay focused on the cross. It is not easy to pray fervently, but we must have confidence that God will hear us and answer us.

III. **Prayer Winners**
If we continue steadfastly in prayer, God will reward our faithfulness. He will always answer us. It might not be what we want to hear, but He will answer. Jesus took time to pray in the wilderness and we must do the same. When we look at all of the promises in God's Word, why worry? Just turn them over to Him and you will win the battle.

APPLICATION: As you pray today say, "Here, Lord, I am casting all my worries on you because you said to do so. I am making a commitment to become a prayer warrior, so I can be a winner. Help me to do so."

WEEK 27—FRIDAY

God Is on Our Side

SCRIPTURE READING: Romans 8:31–39
THREE KEY WORDS: Condemnation—Chosen—Cross

I. Condemnation

Sometimes we not only feel that we should be condemned by God, but also we feel condemned by being Christians. When we take a stand or witness to others, others might make fun of us or we might feel alone, but God says there is no condemnation for those who are in Christ Jesus.

II. Chosen

When we feel alone, we must remember as Christians we were chosen by God, our Father, and Jesus, our Brother, to be in His family. What a privilege to know that I am so special that God chose me to be His son, like Jesus, and that He has prepared a home for me in heaven.

III. Cross

Whenever we feel condemned by God or others here on earth, we must look at the cross and remember that Christ suffered for us so that we would not be condemned. He suffered and died so we could be a part of God's family. We are His chosen, so be grateful. We are not *condemned*, we were *chosen* by Him to be His *children* and that makes us *complete*.

APPLICATION: As you pray today, praise God for being one of His chosen people, created in His image, with no condemnation, no matter what happens. Today and every day will be much brighter when we focus on what resulted from the cross.

WEEK 28—MONDAY

Dying to Live

SCRIPTURE READING: Luke 9:18–26
THREE KEY WORDS: Daily—Denying—Dying

I. Daily
Living for Christ is a daily thing. It is not just a sometime thing. It is an all-the-time thing. Daily we are to arise each morning ready to carry our load, because daily Christ is there with His wonderful grace to strengthen us and to help us carry that load.

II. Denying
To daily live for Christ we must deny our fleshly desires. We must put aside all of our material desires, our desire to have better mates or children, or to live somewhere else, have more money, a better career. "If onlys" in life must be put aside as we surrender our will to God's will.

III. Dying
Daily living for Christ and denying our personal desires means that we must daily die for Christ. We must put to death our own heart's desires and quietly submit to God's will, and say to Him, "Lord, not my will but Your will." Die for Him today.

APPLICATION: As you start your day, ask God to help you to deny yourself, to take up your cross and follow Him no matter where He leads. It is not easy, but it is more rewarding when we deny desires and daily live for Him.

WEEK 28—TUESDAY

Be a Light

SCRIPTURE READING: Ephesians 5:8–14
THREE KEY WORDS: Light—Love—Life

I. Light
As the Bible says in today's scripture, we are to be a light in a darkened world. In today's society where greed, lust and sin are prevalent, it is very difficult to do this. As morals decline and culture is geared toward eating, drinking, and being merry, we must live in the light of Christ. This is why Jesus said to go into the world and be a light, but don't succumb to it.

II. Love
One of the ways we show the light to the world is to show the love of Christ to the world. When we see people living in sin, we should point them towards Christ, the one true light we can live by. We are to be children of light.

III. Life
When we give light to the darkened world, we also give life. Jesus said, "I have come to give life abundant here, but more important, I have come to give eternal life." As I go out today, Lord, help me to be a light for You.

APPLICATION: It is hard to be a light in a darkened world. Remember that if it were easy, everybody would be doing it. Also remember the old saying that you might be the only Bible a person may ever read. Let your light be a shining biblical example today.

WEEK 28—WEDNESDAY

End Revenge

SCRIPTURE READING: Romans 12:9–27
THREE KEY WORDS: Revenge—Repay—Reward

I. Revenge
As we go through life, people are going to do things that anger and hurt us. If we let that stay in our hearts, bitterness will enter and we will seek revenge. It will hurt us more than help us if we seek revenge.

II. Repay
The Lord says that vengeance is His. He is the one to pay back evil for evil. In fact, He instructs us to feed our enemy if he is hungry, give him water if he is thirsty. When we do good to an enemy, he will feel ashamed for what he has done to us.

III. Reward
God says that when we do this, we will receive a reward. He will heal the anger and bitterness and we will feel at peace. We are to conquer evil by doing good; so when people are mean to us, try to be Christ-like to them. Let God do the "get-even" work.

APPLICATION: If you have hard feelings and are angry or bitter toward someone, do as the Bible says and go to that person today or call him and get the matter settled. God says we are to leave the altar and get right with that person before we can continue on. When you do so, God will reward you with the peace that passeth all understanding.

WEEK 28—THURSDAY

Our Hearts

SCRIPTURE READING: Luke 8:5–15
THREE KEY WORDS: Soil—Seeds—Sin

I. Soil
Our hearts are like fertile ground and will produce what we plant there. If we sow seeds of sin, we will produce a bitter heart. If we sow seeds of righteousness, we will reap the Lord's mercy and He will rain blessings upon us. We must have fertile soil in our hearts for God to bless us or we will produce bitterness.

II. Seeds
The natural law of God is that we reap what we sow. When I sow seeds of evil thoughts, lust, or yield to temptations, and let sin control my flesh, my soft soil will turn to hard ground that cannot receive the good seeds that can help me grow. I must yield my soil and heart to God daily.

III. Sin
When we try to control our lives by trying to defeat Satan on our own, Satan will harden our soil. We cannot plant or harvest our godly seeds unless we let God have total control of our hard hearts and let Him daily plow the soil of our hearts through His Word. Yield today.

APPLICATION: As you pray today, ask God for a tender heart. Plant the seed of the gospel as you talk to others today. Ask God to give you the power to overcome sin so your heart will stay soft and loving for Him and others. Today sow seeds of love and kindness.

WEEK 28—FRIDAY

How Deserving Are We?

SCRIPTURE READING: Deuteronomy 9:1–6
THREE KEY WORDS: Deserving—Detrimental—Decision

I. Deserving
As I go through life, I sometimes say to myself that I deserve more. I work harder than anyone I know. Here I am, sixty-one years old and I have to work every day while others I know are retiring. I don't deserve this. I deserve much better. I give a lot of money and time to the Lord. I should get better, I deserve it.

II. Detrimental
This kind of thinking is a sin and is detrimental to our walk with the Lord. What I really deserve is hell, but God loves me so much that He hasn't given me what I deserve. He's given me His grace for living on earth and eternal life instead of eternal death. What a loving God to do this for an undeserving person.

III. Decision
Today I need to decide that I will praise God daily for all of the wonderful gifts He has given me that I don't deserve—health, a great wife and family, and nice material possessions. I don't need more to be thankful for—I need to be more thankful.

APPLICATION: Realize today that we don't really deserve anything we have. That is a fleshly desire and can be detrimental to our walk with God. Then make a decision that because of what Christ did for us on the cross, He deserves our best, because He died for us. That is the least we can do for Him.

WEEK 29—MONDAY
God's Word

SCRIPTURE READING: Psalm 119:121–128
THREE KEY WORDS: Savior—Servant—Success

I. Savior

God sent Jesus His Son to be my savior. Jesus died just for me, he loved me that much. He also wants to bless me, as David said, "Commit yourself to bless me, Lord." I am asking Jesus to bless me abundantly and treat me with loving kindness. Jesus loves me, this I know for the Bible tells me so.

II. Servant

Since Jesus loves me this much, I should serve Him daily as His servant, but in today's world, this is very hard to do. Therefore, Jesus, as I read today's scripture, I am asking you to help this servant to obey. Keep me from sinning. *As your servant, I am asking you to give me common sense to apply your rules to everything I do.*

III. Success

Lord, I want to be a success for you and in my life. Therefore, help me to love Your words more than gold. Make them a part of me. As you say in Psalm 1, if I meditate on it day and night, You will help me prosper. Help me to do so today, Lord.

APPLICATION: As you begin today, thank Jesus for being your savior. Surrender your day to Him to be His servant. Meditate on His Word all day, and I promise you that you will have a successful day.

WEEK 29—TUESDAY

Deceived

SCRIPTURE READING: John 8:34–47
THREE KEY WORDS: Deceived—Destruction—Determined

I. Deceived
Satan makes the temptations of this world look good. Sin is fun and you will enjoy it, but that is only partially true. There is a thrill to cheating on your spouse or going to a topless bar because of the excitement of lust and imagination, but that is a *prescription* for *destruction*.

II. Destruction
If we continue in Satan's deception of sin, we will soon be caught in that sin, and then comes defeat and destruction. We lose our reputations, our friends or family, and we are defeated. We have to start all over again. The question we have to ask ourselves is: "Is one hour of pleasure worth a lifetime of pain?"

III. Determined
We must be determined and make a commitment that we are going to follow God. No matter how strong Satan's deception is, the facts are that "greater is He who is in me than he who is in the world, and true joy is the joy of the Lord." Defeat Satan today.

APPLICATION: If you are going through a battle over sin right now, make a decision to avoid destruction and be determined that no matter what comes your way today, you will resist and flee the evil one and find fellowship with the perfect one. This will bring joy to your day.

WEEK 29—WEDNESDAY

Serving Jesus

SCRIPTURE READING: John 21:15–19
THREE KEY WORDS: Motive—Method—Master

I. Motive

As I sit here today, and after reading the scripture, I have to ask myself, what is my motive for serving Jesus? Is it to bring glory, attention and appreciation from others? Is it to tell my story so people will think I am great or feel sorry for me? Is it my complete love for Christ? I think it could be the earthly rewards I receive. Please forgive me, Jesus. Help my motives to be right.

II. Method

What is my method to serve Jesus? Right now it is telling my story, and I am truly grateful for doing so and for the people who have been won for Christ. What happens, however, to people I meet in everyday life? Is my love strong enough to use a method of simply sitting down and being a witness to them one-on-one? It takes courage to do so.

III. Master

Lord, please restore the joy of salvation. Please bring me back to my first love. Help me to develop a close relationship with you and to love you more than anything in the world. Then, help me to show that love to others.

APPLICATION: All of us have a motive and method to witness for Christ. Ask God to help your motives to be pure and then ask Him for a method that fits your personality to be a witness for Him. He will show you where and how to do so.

WEEK 29—THURSDAY

Battle Praise

SCRIPTURE READING: 2 Chronicles 20:1–22
THREE KEY PHRASES: The Battle—The Believer—The Blessing

I. The Battle
Just as in today's scripture where they fought a great battle, every day we face our own personal battles. We face bad business, finances, loneliness, family problems, health problems, and other things come into our lives where Satan stands between us and God. I feel like I am in a big battle and there is no way out.

II. The Believer
When we face this battle, we are powerless to defend ourselves, but like Jahaziel, we can say as a believer, "The battle is not mine, but God's." I can put on the whole armor of God and turn it over to Him, because when the battle comes, God says that greater is He who is in you than he who is in the world.

III. The Blessing
When we let go and let God, just like the great song says: "It is finished, the battle is over, it is finished, there will be no more war. It is finished, the end of the conflict. It is finished and Jesus is Lord." Let God have your burdens and battles today.

APPLICATION: As we battle through the day as a believer, we must let God have control. When we do, God will pour out His blessings upon us. To keep from getting battle weary, let God fight your battles for you.

WEEK 29—FRIDAY

Misquote

SCRIPTURE READING: Deuteronomy 4:1–14
THREE KEY WORDS: Law—Lie—Lesson

I. **Law**

In today's scripture we see the importance of God's law. God said to Israel, "These are the laws you are to obey. They are from God." God gave us a blueprint to live by today. We are not under the law, but we are to use the law as guidelines to obey God. Even yet today, God says obedience is better than sacrifice.

II. **Lie**

In today's world we hear so many preachers preach about grace, and that grace is a wonderful blessing from God. God showed it was impossible to keep the law so he promised grace, but unfortunately, today there are people adding to the Word of God and not holding to its truth. As it says in the Bible, in the last days you will hear the tickling of the ears. There is a lot of false doctrine today.

III. **Lesson**

God's laws are to teach us lessons for life and He also says that we are to teach these lessons to our children and grandchildren. All the lessons of life are contained in God's Word, but we must discern the truth from lies and obey God's truths.

APPLICATION: As you pray today, thank God for His wonderful grace and that we don't have to live by the letter of the law. Remember, however, that the law is our guideline for everyday Christian living. Ask God to give you the power to do so.

WEEK 30—MONDAY

Shine

SCRIPTURE READING: Matthew 5:14–16
THREE KEY WORDS: Light—Love—Life

I. Light
As a Christian, I am to shine as a light to the world. My testimony should be so bright that other people see Christ in me. Just as the moon reflects the radiance of the sun, we should reflect the light of Christ in our lives.

II. Love
One of the ways we shine for Christ is to love others. We are to love our neighbors as ourselves. One of the greatest qualities of Christ is that He loved common and ordinary people. Even though He was a king, He shared his love with the common and ordinary people. I need to do the same.

III. Life
In life today we are to have balance with purpose, gratitude, and joy. Our purpose should be to win others to Christ, to be a light shining brightly, and to love others as Christ loved the church. We have the Holy Spirit's power in us to do so, so let your light shine by spreading the good news of Christ.

APPLICATION: As you pray today, ask Christ to bring someone into your mind or path who is a good, common, ordinary person. Show love toward that person and let your light shine for Christ today.

WEEK 30—TUESDAY

A Good Name

SCRIPTURE READING: Proverbs 10:1–7
THREE KEY WORDS: Remember—Reflection—Reputation

I. Remember

Occasionally, we should stop and remember the ones who have gone before us and the impact they have had on our lives, such as our parents or grandparents and how much they impacted us with their integrity, their great example of witnessing to others, and how faithful they were through all their struggles. It is important to remember their impact on our lives.

II. Reflection

As we think of these people, we should reflect on their positive attributes and the impact they had on others. Then we also should reflect on how we must do the same for our children and grandchildren, so when we go before them, they can also reflect on how we impacted their lives like those who have gone before us have impacted us.

III. Reputation

To be able to do so, we must keep our good reputation. Solomon said that a good name is to be chosen rather than great riches. Think of people who have faltered and the price they paid, and then think of those who made a positive impact on you through their integrity and character. Then ask yourself, which do you want to leave behind, riches that rust away, or a good reputation that will affect your family for life?

APPLICATION: As you start your day with prayer, take time to meditate and remember your personal Hall of Faith members who made an impact on your life. Reflect on all the good times you had together. Then, ask God to help you be a good example to others.

WEEK 30—WEDNESDAY

Sorrow

SCRIPTURE READING: Ecclesiastes 7:1–14
FOUR KEY WORDS: Struggle—Suffering—Sorrow—Survival

I. Struggle
As we go through the game of life, we are going to face struggles. In fact the older we get, sometimes the harder the struggle. We will have struggles with finances, children, family, health, and marriage, but our *survival* will depend on how we handle *struggle*.

II. Suffering
One of the struggles in life is suffering—emotionally, physically, and spiritually. Suffering can bring a great deal of pain and one of the hardest is when we lose a loved one. This is real suffering.

III. Sorrow
At the time we don't understand how sorrow can be good, but Romans 8:28 is accurate—all things work together for good. It can bring out the best in us if we look to God. We get to know ourselves better. *Sorrow* is *sadness*, but there is *survival*.

IV. Survival
We need to get over sorrow. It will be there for a long time, but survival will come day by day. Finally we will understand it when we see Jesus in heaven.

APPLICATION: If you are going through struggles or suffering right now, ask God to put His arms of love around you. Surrender it all to the Lord. If you are sorrowful, ask for the same help. Then find someone you can talk to. Also focus on the cross and remember that in heaven there are no *struggles*, *suffering*, or *sorrow*. This will help you *survive* the day.

WEEK 30—THURSDAY

Life's Circumstances

SCRIPTURE READING: 1 Corinthians 12:7–10
THREE KEY WORDS: Complain—Compare—Confess

I. Complain

As we go through life's circumstances, one of the biggest struggles I face is complaining. I am always concentrating on the thorns and not the roses. I gripe about my job, where I live, not seeing my family, hard work, not being able to retire, etc. It really comes down to my attitude and my earthly desires.

II. Compare

The complaining comes about because I am always comparing my circumstances to everyone elses'. I look at a lot of my friends who have it made financially and think only of myself. I also compare my hard work with that of others and think "why do I have to work so hard? Why can they take so much time off and go where they want to go and do what they want to do?" But, I don't think of a lot of my friends and people I know who have physical problems such as cancer, heart trouble, etc. I should instead be grateful to God for my health and family.

III. Confess

I need to confess these things to God and let Him take control of my circumstances, to praise Him for what I have and not for what I don't have. I need to take a daily inventory of all my blessings and give my praise to Him. Lord, help me to do so.

APPLICATION: If, like me, you sometimes have the tendency to gripe and complain a great deal, confess it to God and ask Him to forgive you. Then, each day, try your best to focus on all the wonderful blessings God gives you each day. Remember, it is the little things in life that make the biggest difference.

WEEK 30—FRIDAY

Departing

SCRIPTURE READING: John 14:1–6
THREE KEY WORDS: Departure—Duty—Deliverance

I. Departure
Someday we are going to die and go to a place that God has prepared for us. Will it be a blessing or a burden? In other words, if we are born again, it will be a *blessing* for us and the loved ones we leave behind, if not we will cause them a *burden* for life, so make sure you are ready.

II. Duty
If we get the opportunity before we die, it is our duty to give a loving tender blessing to each loved one to encourage them to keep the Lord in the center of their lives. We should also comfort them that someday we will all be together in heaven if they have accepted Christ as their Savior. Our example of how we lived here and the words we say may be the most precious blessing we leave behind.

III. Deliverance
Because we have been delivered from the sting of death through the death, burial, and resurrection of Christ, when we die, it should be a joyous occasion, just like it was when Christ ascended to Heaven. Are we ready?

APPLICATION: Today as you pray, thank God for what Christ did so we can go to heaven. Also remember that not everyone is ready for their judgment. Therefore, it is our duty to find someone we can share the gospel with whenever possible. Ask God to help you do so today.

WEEK 31—MONDAY
Finding Rest

SCRIPTURE READING: Psalm 23
THREE KEY WORDS: Rest—Renewal—Restore

I. Rest
In our everyday busy world, we need to find time to rest. As in the Psalm today, we need to take a walk along the green meadows next to the creek and enjoy the Lord's creation, but our true daily rest must come from God alone and our relationship with Him. We need to let Him take control of everything we do to really find rest.

II. Renewal
When we do this, it will renew our strength and also our faith. Just like we renew our relationships with family and friends, we need to renew our relationship with our Father. The only way to do that is to find the time to rest in Him.

III. Restore
As the Psalm said today, God will restore our souls. I sometimes pray, "God, restore unto me the joy of my salvation. Give me that joy and bring desire once again." When I *rest* in Him, and *renew* my faith, God will *restore* my soul. Lord, help me to do so starting today.

APPLICATION: The best way to start your day and every day is to simply rest on the promises of God. His Word is full of them. Look up the word "promise" in your concordance and read a few scriptures. When you do, it will renew your strength and restore your soul.

WEEK 31—TUESDAY

Taste the Goodness of God

SCRIPTURE READING: Psalm 33
THREE KEY WORDS: Goodness—Grace—Gratitude

I. Goodness
When things are tough in our lives, we need to do as the Psalmist did and say, "I will praise the Lord no matter what happens. I will continually speak of His glories and grace." We must realize during our trials that God is good. We need to ask ourselves, how could we make it through without the goodness of God? We need to remember Romans 8:28 and realize that all things are good.

II. Grace
We also need to remember not only the goodness of God, but the grace of God and His mercy. The fact that we don't have to earn our salvation, but through His grace He loves us enough to have sent Jesus who died for our sins. Oh, what wonderful grace.

III. Gratitude
In all of these things we can show our *gratitude* and *gratefulness* by living for Him. Life is tough, but when we focus on God's *goodness* and *grace*, we should be so *grateful* and show our *gratitude* daily to Him.

APPLICATION: As you start this new day, have an attitude of gratitude. Be thankful for God's goodness and grace and then share your gratitude by simply thanking and praising Him for being in your life.

WEEK 31—WEDNESDAY

Our Helpers

SCRIPTURE READING: Hebrews 1
THREE KEY WORDS: Angels—Appearance—Answers

I. Angels
In today's scripture, God talks about angels. They serve Christ, but they have an important ministry. They are spirit messengers sent out to help and care for us when we are in need. Each of us has our own angel who watches over us and helps us when God tells them to do so.

II. Appearance
When Jesus was tempted by Satan, the Bible says angels came and ministered to Him. They appeared to Him. Angels will not appear to us, but we will sense them with our spirit. It might be through the Word, or some significant or insignificant person or happening that takes place in our life. We will sense their presence when they appear.

III. Answers
Sometimes when my spirit or body is really hurting and I pray fervently for help, God sends my angel to minister to me and brings answers to my prayers. God uses angels to be my real helpers in times of need, and He will do the same for you.

APPLICATION: If you are having a tough time right now, ask God to minister to those personal needs by sending you an angel as He did for Jesus. It might be through His Word, a person or circumstances, so you also need to ask Him for a sensitive spirit to recognize the angel when it does appear.

WEEK 31—THURSDAY
The Road of Life

SCRIPTURE READING: John 16:19–33
THREE KEY WORDS: Rough—Rocky—Repair

I. Rough
As we go through life, we are going to hit some rough roads, and some deep ruts. Jesus said that if we follow Him this could happen. We will have rough roads with finances, health, business, and family, but Jesus is the one to take the ruts we face and help us to make it through. Without Him, we can do nothing.

II. Rocky
Not only will our road be rough, but also it will be rocky. We will face ups and downs as we ride the highway of life. There will be high points and low points; Jesus will help us enjoy the highs and make it through the lows if we just turn to Him.

III. Repair
As we ride the road of life and hit the rough and rocky points, we will also have some severe cracks in our lives, but Jesus is there to repair these cracks and make them smooth again. The hurts and sorrows will also be healed someday when we are united with Him. Remember, the roads in heaven are all smooth and made of gold.

APPLICATION: If you are riding a rough and rocky road in life right now, ask the Lord to help you make it through. If you have hurts and cracks in your heart as a result, ask Him to repair your heart as well. Then, remember all of the faithful people in the Hall of Faith in Hebrews 11 and the rewards they now have. It will help you through these rough and rocky times.

WEEK 31—FRIDAY

Truth

SCRIPTURE READING: 2 Chronicles 18:1–7
THREE KEY WORDS: Truth—Trouble—Tragedy

I. Truth
The only thing that passes the test of time is truth. As we look at our country today, there is no black and white, it is all gray area. As I look at my own life, I try very hard to be truthful, but sometimes I exaggerate, or bend the truth to meet my needs. God says I need to deal with that because it is a sin. I need to turn to the truth of His Word and be truthful daily no matter what comes into my life.

II. Trouble
When we are not truthful, we will eventually get into trouble. As the scriptures say, "Be sure your sins will find you out." Just like little kids tell white lies that eventually get them into trouble, the same will happen to us. As the Bible says, truth will not only keep us out of trouble, but it will set us free.

III. Tragedy
Eventually our troubles will become tragedy. Just look at the religious and business world, politics, sports—there is a battlefield of wounded notables who have gone through great tragedies because they were not truthful. We can prevent trouble and tragedy by letting truth guide our lives.

APPLICATION: If a situation takes place in your life today that causes you to have to choose between the truth or a lie, remember there is no option with God. You must always be truthful. He will reward you for your faithfulness and truthfulness.

WEEK 32—MONDAY

Pride

SCRIPTURE READING: 1 John 2:15–17
THREE KEY WORDS: Humiliated—Hurt—Humble

I. Humiliated
As we live our lives day by day, things happen that can humiliate us. It might be taking a stand for Christ at work and being made fun of for it, or it could be a presentation we give that somebody criticizes, or some family matter like our kids doing something wrong to embarrass us. Humiliation is hard to face.

II. Hurt
When this happens, we suffer hurt. It might be hurt feelings, or sincere hurt in our hearts, but most of the time, it is our pride that gets hurt. We can get angry and want to get even to relieve the hurt, but that is not God's way.

III. Humble
God says unless we are humble, we're sure to stumble. He says do not love the things of the world—sins, material possessions, promotions—that can cause pride. God resists the proud but gives grace to the humble. We need to remember the humiliation that Jesus suffered on the cross to help us resist pride and be humble.

APPLICATION: If something or someone has caused you humiliation and hurt, ask God to heal your heart. If you are suffering from pride right now, ask Him to forgive you and to help you be humble. It is hard to do sometimes, but remember God's promise that He gives grace to the humble.

WEEK 32—TUESDAY

Trouble with People

SCRIPTURE READING: Psalm 56
THREE KEY WORDS: Trouble—Temptation—Trust

I. Trouble
Many times we face fear and trouble in our lives because of what other people say about us or things they try to do to us. They tell lies and backbite; they may even be so angry with us that it causes us trouble in our minds and spirit. Life is full of troubles, and many times they are caused by others.

II. Temptation
When this happens, we may be tempted to quit trying, or we might want to get even with them, but God says vengeance is mine. So when people cause us trouble, turn to God for help.

III. Trust
When all of this piles up in our lives, we need to turn to and trust God. What can a mere man to do me? If God is for me, who can be against me? So when trouble comes into my life and I get tempted to give up, I need to turn to God and trust Him completely.

APPLICATION: If someone has caused trouble in your life and you are tempted to get even, don't do it. The Bible says to go to that person and make it right. Then trust Him completely to make it right.

WEEK 32—WEDNESDAY

Heart to Heart

SCRIPTURE READING: Psalm 62
THREE KEY PHRASES: The Creator—The Counselor—The Commitment

I. The Creator

God is the great Creator. He created everything for us, around us and in us. He created all of us for a *purpose*, a *profession* and a *people*. My ministry at the drug rehab center has given me a strong purpose the past eleven years. I love the people God created for our ministry. They also have a purpose, and that is remembering that God created them to help others with drug problems.

II. The Counselor

In Psalm 62, David said, "My soul is greatly confident before God." How could David say this with all he faced? I told God this morning, "I am tired, I am weary and alone. I am at the end of my rope. I want to quit and give up. I have fought the battle long." Then I read that God said, "I am your great counselor in everything you say, do, feel and need. I will be your helper."

III. The Commitment

As I go through the day, I have to ask myself am I committed to go on? It all starts with me. Am I committed to build greater unity in my business, church, and family? Am I committed to serving God no matter what? To do so, I need daily contact with the counselor through prayer.

APPLICATION: The Bible says that we are created in God's image. Therefore, we must try our best to live for Him daily. If we need His help, the counselor is always there. Make a commitment today to be your best, no matter what you face.

WEEK 32—THURSDAY

Getting Old

SCRIPTURE READING: Psalm 71
THREE KEY PHRASES: The Aged—The Abandoned—The Appreciated

I. The Aged

As we get older and tired, and our "parts" are wearing out, we can still be used by God. We have to set the path for the younger generation—*family, friends, foes*—and especially our grandchildren. They will walk the paths we walked, fight the battles we fought, so we have to be an example. We also can continue to pray for and encourage others.

II. The Abandoned

Unfortunately, many of our great elderly Christians are put into nursing homes by families that don't have time for them. They feel lonely and that nobody really cares. Sometimes they may even be mistreated physically and mentally. How sad.

III. The Appreciated

Part of our ministry as we get older is to appreciate the elderly, to visit nursing homes, send them cards, and call them, because it won't be long and we will be there as well. Lord, help me to appreciate the "golden saints." Based on my sixty-plus years on this earth, I can say it will happen faster than you think.

Application: As you pray today, ask God to give you compassion for the elderly. Next, make a commitment that you will visit an elderly person this week in a hospital or nursing home. Take a gift or card when you do and it will make your day.

WEEK 32—FRIDAY

Something to Say

SCRIPTURE READING: Isaiah 50
THREE KEY PHRASES: Our Message—Our Mind—Our Meditation

I. Our Message
Each day as I open God's Word, I should look for a message that I can apply to my life. That is why I wrote these mini-messages so I can use them throughout the day. God also wants me to take these messages and encourage the weary. I am weary each day and I need to encourage them with God's Word.

II. Our Mind
Each day, when I open God's Word, I should be eager to learn something new that I can put in my mind and heart. We can transform our mind by blocking everything else out and asking God to not only speak to our hearts but also our minds.

III. Our Meditation
When finished reading God's message and filling our mind with God's Word, we should take time to meditate on the message until we know how He wants us to apply it to our lives. Once we find out, we should use that message to encourage others.

APPLICATION: As you read Isaiah 50 today, ask God to speak to your heart and mind in a special way. Look for words that speak to you. Meditate on the message, then apply it by giving it to someone else. This is how we can encourage others.

WEEK 33—MONDAY

Faith Is Enough

SCRIPTURE READING: Isaiah 6:8–13
THREE KEY PHRASES: Faithfulness—Frightfulness—Fruitfulness

I. Faithfulness

The world crowns success but God crowns faithfulness. As we go out to live in the real world each day, we fight a lot of the devil's temptation (work is too hard, I will never make it, if only I had more money, etc.) but God expects us to be faithful to His Word and His call. God is faithful to do abundantly more than we could even ask or think. Remember this daily.

II. Frightfulness

As we go out and fight the battle each day, it can be fearful. We confront *people, problems,* or *persecution.* People think we are crazy for following Christ, problems in relationships come as a result, persecution hurts. Remember His *promise*—I will never leave you nor forsake you.

III. Fruitfulness

If we are faithful and never give up, we will be fruitful. God's Word will not return void; obedience is better than sacrifice. Eventually by being faithful, someone will listen, and we will bear fruit. Lord, help me to be faithful today.

APPLICATION: If you know someone you need to witness to but are fearful to do so, ask God to give you the strength. Be faithful to His promise that if you plant the seed, He will reap the harvest and you will see fruit. Don't be *frightful*, be *fruitful*.

WEEK 33—TUESDAY

What We Really Need

SCRIPTURE READING: Proverbs 3:13–26
THREE KEY WORDS: Wisdom—Wealth—Witness

I. Wisdom

The key word in life to be *happy, healthy* and *humble* is wisdom. The Bible says that if we know right from wrong, have good judgment and common sense, that we are happier than all of the rich people of the world. In fact, it says that we should only have two goals—wisdom and common sense. Everything else will have meaning for us.

II. Wealth

A lot of people have no wisdom or happiness. Just look at all of the athletes today who make hundreds of millions of dollars right out of high school. What do they know? Nothing. In fact, with all their wealth, many will be miserable and end up on drugs. Money does not make us wealthy, wisdom gives us wealth in every area of life.

III. Witness

With wisdom, we can be great witnesses. We can help and meet the needs of others and also keep our own lives in order. Please, Lord, more than anything else give me wisdom and love.

APPLICATION: God promises that if we ask for wisdom, He will give to all men liberally. Wisdom is the beginning of knowledge. God will also give us wisdom to witness when we need to do so. As the Bible says, seek wisdom and you will receive great riches. You will find that you will prosper in every area of your life.

WEEK 33—WEDNESDAY

On Loan

SCRIPTURE READING: Psalm 89:1–12
THREE KEY PHRASES: Our Possessions—Our Provider—Our Purpose

I. Our Possessions

Everything we have in life—our time, talents, material possessions such as house, cars, furniture, even our kids and grandkids—absolutely everything is on loan while we are here on earth. It all belongs to God. Someday, when we die, we will leave behind all of these possessions. Also, our most important possessions such as our family and friends will be with us for all eternity in heaven.

II. Our Provider

The Lord has provided all of these wonderful things for us. He has given us the time and talent to enjoy all these wonderful possessions while here on earth. We are to be good stewards of what He has provided us. As Solomon said, all that really matters is that we love and praise God. It all comes down to *faith, family,* and *friendships.*

III. Our Purpose

Our purpose in all that the Lord has provided us is to prepare us and our loved ones for heaven. How sad it would be if we get to heaven and our most prized possessions—kids, grandkids, and friends—are not there with us. Be sure you use all that God has provided you with to see them in heaven.

APPLICATION: As you start your day, thank and praise God for all of your wonderful possessions and blessings—material, physical, mental, financial and spiritual. Next, remember your purpose and ask the provider for help to carry out that purpose.

WEEK 33—THURSDAY
Hold on to God

SCRIPTURE READING: Psalm 91
THREE KEY PHRASES: Hold on to God—Hope in God—Help from God

I. Hold on to God
Like a ship in a rough sea, or a car traveling up a steep hill, or when we climb a steep stairway, we need something to hold onto to steady us. The game of life is rocky and rough, and if we don't trust God and hold onto Him, we can go down like a ship in rough seas. So hold on.

II. Hope in God
For Christians, when we go through troubles, there is hope in God. Our hope is found in nothing less than Jesus Christ and righteousness when we put our hope in God. We have someone we can rely on in every circumstance in life. He is our hope.

III. Help from God
God has not promised to keep us from life's storms, but to help us through them. God is always there to help us when we need hope and strength. He is a refuge and fortress, a very present help in time of need, so we need to hold on, hope in, trust Him, and He will help us to weather the storm.

APPLICATION: If times are tough for you right now and you are going through a stormy period, ask God to help you to hold on. Nobody had a rougher ride in the storm than Jonah in the whale, but even in that hopeless situation, God came through and He will do the same for you.

WEEK 33—FRIDAY
Limitations

SCRIPTURE READING: Exodus 4:10–12
THREE KEY WORDS: Limitations—Lessons—Love

I. Limitations
When God asks us to do something as He asked Moses in today's scripture, we put limitations on ourselves. We tell ourselves, "I don't have the ability or knowledge to do what the Lord has asked", or "I am not worthy," but just as God worked supernaturally through Moses, He also can work supernaturally through us. There are no limitations to what we can do if we will surrender to God.

II. Lessons
God tells us to do something and shows us how to do it. When He works supernaturally through our lives, we learn lessons from Him. We are then to take these lessons and use them as examples to teach others how God can work through them as well.

III. Love
God loves us so much that He wants to use us to love others without limitations. Like Paul, we should realize that our limitations don't limit us because as he said, "When I am weak, then I am strong and God can use me beyond my limitations." As the Word says, we can do more than you can imagine or think.

APPLICATION: Most of our limitations are self-imposed. God has no limitations for us when we surrender everything in our life to Him. Take the lessons you have learned from life, ask God to use you in a supernatural way to love others, and you can go farther than you ever dreamed you could. Enjoy the ride!

WEEK 34—MONDAY

Standing Before God

SCRIPTURE READING: 1 Corinthians 5:1–11
THREE KEY WORDS: Judgment—Justice—Joy

I. Judgment
Someday, when we die, we will all stand before Jesus and give an account of the good, the bad, and the ugly. It says in the scripture today that our lives will be laid before Him. Our work will be rewarded and our rewards determined by Him. We will be morally and spiritually audited. This should cause us to live for Him daily.

II. Justice
Because of what Jesus did for us on the cross, justice will be served. God couldn't have been a fair judge if Jesus had not gone to the cross, and then resurrected so we could make the choice of heaven or hell. It is our choice as to what we receive on judgment day. This is justice.

III. Joy
For those who have been born again and lived for Him, that will not only be a day of judgment, but a day of joy. We will receive our new bodies, our new homes, and be with Jesus forever. What joy. Our salvation depends on what Christ did for us. Our rewards depend on what we do for Him. This is justice.

APPLICATION: If there is sin in your life right now that causes you guilt and shame, confess it to Jesus so you won't feel guilty or afraid when you see Him. Remember, when you stand before Him, you will say Lord, I am glad I did or I wished I had settled that issue today.

WEEK 34—TUESDAY

Every Inch of Me

SCRIPTURE READING: Acts 27:13–26
THREE KEY WORDS: Master—Message—Motive

I. Master

As I go out each day, I want Jesus to be my master in all I do. I want to be a witness for Him, so people will see Him in me. They know that I love Him and serve Him because of what He did for me on the cross. Lord, help me to follow you today.

II. Message

I also want the message of Jesus to be seen in me as a living example. There is an old saying that I might be the best Bible somebody will read. The message is so simple, yet so important because it is our only hope for the future.

III. Motive

My motive must be pure and our motivation must be to keep people out of hell. Before her recent death, Katherine Hepburn said she wasn't afraid of hell and didn't think she would like heaven. Well, unless someone got to her with the *message* about the *master*, she is *miserable* for all eternity. How sad. We must get the *message* of the *master* to the *millions* who have not heard.

APPLICATION: Today and every day, make Jesus your master. Take the message of the master to people you know today and ask Him to make your motive pure. Time is running out.

WEEK 34—WEDNESDAY

Kindness

SCRIPTURE READING: Proverbs 19:17–22
THREE KEY WORDS: Others—Ourselves—Opportunity

I. Others

If a catastrophe takes place and people are in need, the question is: Do we help others as ourselves? Jesus would always help others. We should never take advantage of a situation to benefit us, but we should always be kind and helpful to others. When you see a need, ask yourself, What would Jesus do?

II. Ourselves

Because our world is greedy nowadays, people are always putting themselves ahead of others. The flesh says, Give me all I can get. I want what is best for me. I am not worried about tomorrow. We put ourselves first when we should put others first. As it says in the scripture today, kindness makes a man attractive, and it is better to be poor than dishonest.

III. Opportunity

Each day we have an opportunity to be kind to others. As we go out each day, give a little kindness. Meet a need. One of the best ways to do so is to just smile and be friendly to others.

APPLICATION: As you begin your day, start with the following prayer: "Others, Lord, others. Let this my motto be. That I might live for others and more like Jesus be." Then, go do it.

WEEK 34—THURSDAY

Strange Territory

SCRIPTURE READING: Joshua 3:1–13
THREE KEY WORDS: Territory—Terrified—Trust

I. Territory

Many times as we go through life, we have to go into new, strange and unfamiliar territory. It might be a new job, a new city, a new relationship, and we have so much uncertainty for the future. In my own life, that has happened many times—Bloomington to Dallas, Dallas to Denver—new job, new friends, new circumstances, so I understand.

II. Terrified

When these instances take place in our lives, we can be scared and afraid. The old saying that fear of the unknown is still the greatest fear of all rings true in these circumstances. It is or can be a *terrifying* experience or it can be a *terrific* experience. It all depends on where we are in our faith.

III. Trust

When these circumstances and feelings take place, the only thing we can do is to trust God completely. We need to place our trust in Him and walk by faith and remember that He has said that He will never leave us nor forsake us, and that all things work together for God, therefore we need to put our total trust in God each day.

APPLICATION: If you are terrified or afraid of what is taking place in your life right now, put your total trust in God. Ask Him for the peace that passeth all understanding. He will hear your cry and answer. Remember, He said, "I have not given you a spirit of fear, but of power and love and a sound mind." That says it all.

WEEK 34—FRIDAY

Are You Listening?

SCRIPTURE READING: Isaiah 3:1–10
THREE KEY WORDS: Hear—Hindrances—Help

I. Hear
As we let God speak to us each day, we need to ask Him to help us to hear what He is saying. We need to take the time to listen. Like little Samuel did, we need to open our hearts and just say, Lord, speak to my heart today. As a man thinketh in his heart, so is he. We change our hearts by listening to God's Word and applying it to our hearts.

II. Hindrances
One of my biggest problems are all the hindrances that Satan brings into my life as I read God's Word. I think about things I have to get done today or problems I have or people I need to call. The everyday busy things that we allow to interrupt our precious time with God hinders our prayers and hinders God's answers.

III. Help
As we read and pray each day, we need to ask God to help us to block out the hindrances and let the Word go directly to our hearts. Then we need to say, Lord, how can I take what you said today and go help someone else? This is how we can be an example like Jesus, by hearing and then doing.

APPLICATION: A suggestion I can make that has helped me greatly is to have a specific time and place for prayer and worship. I call mine the secret place. As I go to work early each morning, my first prayer is, "Lord, help me block out everything but you for the next hour and stay totally focused on you." Sometimes I start by singing a praise song to get my spirit in tune to His. Sometimes I stand, kneel, walk around, or do all of these. Whatever it takes, don't miss God's voice.

WEEK 35—MONDAY

Encouragement

SCRIPTURE READING: Deuteronomy 3:23–29
THREE KEY WORDS: Encouragement—Effort—Expression

I. **Encouragement**

As we go through life each day, we all need to receive and give words of encouragement. I have heard it said that millions of people go to bed each night starving for food, but tens of millions go to bed each night starving for some type of acceptance or appreciation. We need to meet that need daily.

II. **Effort**

Each day as we go about our business, we really need to make an effort to encourage others. It could be a call, a note or card, or even a small gift. Think of a friend or relative you could encourage today and do it.

III. **Expression**

Encouragement is our expression of love or appreciation for what this person means to us or how they have helped us to make it each day. Today make an effort to express your love to others through words of encouragement. We can never give too much appreciation for what people mean to us. Be an encourager.

APPLICATION: For thirty years now, I have carried a list of five people who I call once a week to give a word of encouragement. I have called one person weekly for twenty-five years. I can't tell you what a blessing it has been in my life. Think of three to five people you know who need encouragement. Put their names on a list and call or write them once a week for four weeks. I promise you that it will not only encourage them, but you will be more encouraged as well.

WEEK 35—TUESDAY

God Is Everywhere

SCRIPTURE READING: Psalm 39
THREE KEY PHRASES: God is Listening—God is Leading—God is Loving

I. God Is Listening

An amazing thought is the fact that when we talk to or about God, He is always listening. We can't say something behind His back about Him; therefore, in all of our discussions, we should realize that God is there. That in itself should keep us from gossiping, lying, or telling off-color jokes. We should talk as if God is in the room, because He is.

II. God Is Leading

The Bible says today that God saw me before Jesus was born, and that He scheduled each day of my life. Every day is decided in His book; therefore I should be willing to trust God and let Him lead by his schedule and not my own. God is leading you and me.

III. God Is Loving

God loved me so much that He made all of my delicate parts and knit them together in my mother's womb. He is constantly thinking about me, and when I get up in the morning, He is still thinking about me. That is so hard for me to fathom. Lord, help me to follow your leading today. Help me to listen for you today, but also to think about you all day today.

APPLICATION: As you converse with others today, remember God is listening. Therefore, ask Him to help you to speak the truth. Also, ask Him to help you control your tongue, and to say things that will bring glory to His name. Be the leader in doing so, and remember God will love you for it.

WEEK 35—WEDNESDAY

Be Thankful

SCRIPTURE READING: Psalm 147
THREE KEY WORDS: Brokenhearted—Burdens—Blessings

I. Brokenhearted
There are a lot of people hurting today. They are brokenhearted because of losing a loved one, a divorce, an illness, or a child going astray and they are hurting. But God says in today's scripture that He heals the brokenhearted, so we need to give Him our hearts.

II. Burdens
Because of this and other problems in life, we carry a lot of burdens. What am I going to do about paying my bills, my kids, my sickness, how can I make it through another day and the daily tasks? Our burdens are so heavy for us and weigh us down.

III. Blessings
One of the best ways to heal our broken hearts and carry our burdens is to take a few minutes and remember all of God's wonderful blessings—our health, home, job, finances, relationships, and all of the miracles we have seen. Lord, please help me to focus on your blessings today.

APPLICATION: One of my favorite songs is titled, *Mending Broken People*. It starts out by saying, "I want to spend my life mending broken people / I want to spend my life just healing pain." That is exactly what Jesus did and we should do the same. Think of someone you know who is brokenhearted, and ask God to give you a burden for that person. Then, go be a blessing to that person. That's what Jesus would do.

WEEK 35—THURSDAY
The Sound of Music

SCRIPTURE READING: Psalm 149
THREE KEY WORDS: Music—Motivate—Minister

I. **Music**

One of the greatest blessings we have in life is music. Like a lot of things, it can be used for good or bad purposes. The world today has ruined music in many ways, but God's people have been so blessed with great hymns and choruses. We need to use God's music as a way to give praises to him.

II. **Motivate**

Music can also be a great motivator. When we are down and out and feeling blue, one of the best ways to get back up again is by listening to some upbeat praise and worship songs. I promise you that it will lift your spirits.

III. **Minister**

Music is also a great minister. When we are spiritually dry and problems overwhelm us, Satan is on the attack. Music can soothe our spirits, just like it did for Saul when David played the harp. God can really minister to us through great music. In the presence of Jehovah, God Almighty, Prince of Peace, trouble vanishes. Hearts are mended in the presence of the King.

APPLICATION: At home or in your car as you go to work, play some good praise and worship music. Sing praises to the Lord. Lift your hands to Him (not in the car, of course) and let the music minister to your soul. I promise you it will be a great motivator and minister.

WEEK 35—FRIDAY

Heaven—Our New Location

SCRIPTURE READING: Philippians 1:12–26
THREE KEY WORDS: Location—Life—Love

I. Location

Living here on earth is our location for a while. We might live in several places like I have, but our final location is far better than here. If we think things are beautiful here, just wait. We will see that nothing can come close to the beauty and joy of our new location in heaven.

II. Life

Life on earth has the good, the bad and the ugly. We have wonderful memories and fun-filled times, but there are bad times as well with family, health problems, finances, etc. This is the way life is here, but not in heaven. There, we will have no more sorrow, pain, suffering, or bad times. We will only have good—no bad or ugly.

III. Love

God loved us so much that He sent Jesus to provide our new location to us. What love He showed when He suffered for us to keep us out of the worst location—hell—and give us a glorious mansion in heaven with our Father. Thank you, Jesus, for paying my price for heaven.

APPLICATION: Remember as you live your life today, that where you are now is only your temporary location. Our final location will be either heaven or hell. It is our choice. Make sure you are ready for heaven and then go forth and get someone else ready as well.

WEEK 36—MONDAY
Trends for Today

SCRIPTURE READING: Proverbs 1:12–26
THREE KEY WORDS: Trends—Tensions—Tradition

I. Trends
There are a lot of things in life that are trendy—dress, hair style, even communication. We communicate in many different ways—by letter, email, phone, and of course, face-to-face. How we communicate with others through our tone of voice and body language will cause them to respond in certain ways. It is hard, but the wisdom of Proverbs says a soft answer turns away wrath, but harsh words cause quarrels. Speak softly, but carry a big stick.

II. Tensions
When we communicate and how we communicate causes responses or reactions in others. Responding is positive and gentle in nature; reacting is negative and can be loud and harsh because people tense up. Let's communicate in ways that reduce tension.

III. Tradition
Trends and tradition can cause tension too. We are set in our ways and we don't like our good old traditions to change, but the fact is that trends in every area of life do change and we establish new traditions. So don't get all tensed up, just relax and turn it over to God.

APPLICATION: The only thing that has not changed and will not change is Jesus. The Bible says, "He is the same yesterday, today, and forever." If change in trends is causing you tension, then follow the old tradition of giving it to the one who never changes, Jesus, and He will give you peace.

WEEK 36—TUESDAY

The Effects of Sin

SCRIPTURE READING: Galatians 6:6–10
THREE KEY WORDS: Particular—Pathetic—Permanent

I. **Particular**

There are particular things in life that are simple black and white issues. One is sowing and reaping. If we sow particular seeds of sin, we will reap particular crops of *problems* that will last a lifetime. If we sow particular seeds of goodness, we will reap a harvest of *praise*.

II. **Pathetic**

It is pathetic to see good people who have scars for life because of planting the wrong seeds and reaping a pathetic seed of sorrow. Remember that when we are tempted to sow seeds of sin, ask yourself, Is it worth the *scars, sorrow,* and *sadness* it will bring to others?

III. **Permanent**

Both seeds have a permanent harvest. Seeds of sin will send us to hell or, for the Christian, will leave us with permanent scars. Seeds of the Savior will send us to heaven and help us here to have the abundant life Christ wants for us. Plant good seeds today.

APPLICATION: If you are dealing with certain sins in your life, confess them to God and receive forgiveness. Then, ask the Holy Spirit to give you power to sow seeds of goodness. Remember, as you sow so shall you also reap. Sow seeds of goodness today.

WEEK 36—WEDNESDAY

Load Limits

SCRIPTURE READING: 1 Corinthians 10:1–13
THREE KEY PHRASES: Load Limits—Lord's Limits—Lesson Limits

I. **Load Limits**
As we go through the game of life, we have load limits to deal with daily: speed limits on the road, limits on weight, like elevators as well as our own bodies, but the biggest load limits we deal with daily are our sins—emotional limits—fleshly limits—stress limits. Just as roads or elevators will collapse under stress and overloads, the same can happen to us.

II. **Lord's Limits**
When we turn everything over to the Lord, then limits are light. Take my yoke upon you for my burdens are easy and my loads are light. Casting all your cares upon Him, because He cares for you. I can do far above anything you ask or think. The Lord knows no limits. He can carry it all if we will only let Him.

III. **Lesson Limits**
The Lord brings loads into our lives to teach us lessons, but for me, I am always trying to do it myself, so I have to learn everything the hard way. Many times I collapse under the load. But the lesson is always the same—trust in the Lord with all your heart and lean not on your own understanding. Lighten your load today. Let the Lord carry it for you.

APPLICATION: If you are all stressed out and the load is so heavy that you could collapse at any time, say a simple prayer and tell the Lord you can't carry it any longer. He has no limits and His love will lighten your load. Give it to Him today.

WEEK 36—THURSDAY

Dare to Be Daniel

SCRIPTURE READING: Daniel 6:1–10
THREE KEY WORDS: Convictions—Compromise—Courage

I. Convictions

As Christians and as leaders, we must have strong convictions. Like Daniel, our convictions must be scriptural and we should not make them as *legalists,* but as *leaders* and *lovers* of the Lord and His Words. People should be able to look at our lives and know what we stand for. Take a stand and live accordingly.

II. Compromise

One of the things that bothers me the most is the fact that I have compromised my convictions over the years with music, television, language, church, etc. Our churches today have also compromised in these areas and I think it has hurt the Christian and the church. We must get back to the Word, the truth, and the standards that God has set for us.

III. Courage

It takes a great deal of courage to live by convictions, but we must stay the course. God will lead us and reward us if we do. He says He gives strength when we need it, and we need it when we take a strong stand for our beliefs. Lord, help me to be like Daniel to have *convictions*, not *compromise*, but have *courage* to stay the *course*.

APPLICATION: If there are some areas in your life where you have compromised your standards or love for Christ, ask Him to forgive you and make a commitment to live by the standards set forth in the word. Ask Him for the hope and power to do so.

WEEK 36—FRIDAY

It Is Okay to Cry

SCRIPTURE READING: Lamentations 3
THREE KEY WORDS: Tears—Troubles—Triumph

I. Tears

When tragedy or sorrow comes into our lives, it is okay to shed some tears. Even though Jesus never sinned, he still had feelings, and sometimes sorrow, sadness, and even sickness of others gave him a heavy heart. In fact, the shortest verse in the Bible simply says, "Jesus wept." It is not a sign of weakness to cry. In fact, it is a sign of real strength that in the flesh we can't make it, but with God's help we can.

II. Troubles

In life, we face troubles. This is a fact. They might even be daily troubles, like facing sickness, or stress on the job, trouble with kids, and the weight just gets so heavy that we can't bear it. One of the ways to feel better is just to get alone with God, pour out your heart to Him and have a good cry.

III. Triumph

Some day when this life is over, we won't have to face tragedy or troubles and we won't shed tears of sadness, but tears of joy. In fact, the Bible says in Revelations 2:14 that Jesus himself will wipe away all tears. It will be worth it all when we see Jesus.

APPLICATION: As you pray today, take your tears of sadness and turn them into tears of joy by letting Jesus simply love you. Remember His promise that there is nothing too difficult for Him to handle, and also remember that because of His triumph over the grave, we will have no tears or troubles in heaven.

WEEK 37—MONDAY

What Will Last?

SCRIPTURE READING: 2 Corinthians 4:16–18
THREE KEY PHRASES: The Past—The Present—The Permanent

I. **The Past**
   As we look back on all the years of our lives, there are different things that we thought were so important, but as we look at them today, we realize they were not that important after all. It could have been a possession or relationship that we thought would bring happiness forever, but it didn't last so we moved on.

II. **The Present**
   As we live our present lives, we should learn from these lessons and concentrate on what is important today, what will bring lasting results and not temporary results. We can become so caught up in ourselves and what will bring us happiness now that we forget about eternity.

III. **The Permanent**
   The only thing that is permanent is what we do for Christ. Only what is done for Christ will last. As we look at the *past* and *present*, let's *prepare* for the *permanent*—our home in heaven and being with Jesus forever.

APPLICATION: As you start your day, think about your past and some of the lessons you have learned that can help you live better in the present. Then try to take these lessons you learned and make them permanent for your future. Also pass the lessons on to your children and grandchildren.

WEEK 37—TUESDAY
Unexpected Grief

SCRIPTURE READING: 2 Corinthians 1:1–11
THREE KEY WORDS: Grief—Goodness—Godliness

I. Grief
As we live life each day, month, and year, there are going to be times when we experience grief. In most cases, it is unexpected and we aren't prepared. It could be a sudden death, serious illness, loss of job, or a child gone astray. The hardest thing of all is how we handle it.

II. Goodness
When we suffer grief, we must always remember the goodness of God. It isn't easy, but Romans 8:28 is God's Word. We don't understand how good can come from grief, but it will. Christ is the one who comforts and strengthens us. We must put everything into His hands and He will comfort us and show His love and mercy toward us.

III. Godliness
Part of going through grief might be to make us more godly—to let go and let God. To put Him first in everything we do. To trust in the Lord with all our heart and lean not on our own understanding, but cast all our cares on Him because He cares for us. When *grief* comes, remember God's *goodness*, and try to remain *godly*.

APPLICATION: If you are personally going through grief right now, seek help from someone you know or a grief counselor. I also suggest that you read a tremendous book by Zig Ziglar titled, *Confession of a Grieving Christian*, written after his daughter passed away. If you know someone who is going through grief, go and minister to that person and take Zig's book with you.

WEEK 37—WEDNESDAY

Obsolete

SCRIPTURE READING: Isaiah 35
THREE KEY WORDS: Sorrow—Sadness—Solution

I. Sorrow

Here on earth we have a lot of sorrow in our lives. We lose a loved one or a tragedy happens in our family, we feel lonely and depressed and sorrow fills our souls. We sometimes have to sigh just to get relief. Sorrow is a heavy burden that we sometimes carry for a long time.

II. Sadness

Another sign of sorrow is when it gets too heavy that we live in a state of sadness. Life is so unbearable, we feel like there is no light at the end of the tunnel. Tears fall upon our pillow at night when we are alone; and sadness is such a lonely world.

III. Solution

No matter how much sorrow we have or sadness we bear, we have the assurance that someday because of our salvation that sorrow and sadness will be obsolete. Jesus said, no more *sickness, sadness,* or *sorrow* when we get to heaven, only *sunshine, singing,* and *happiness* will fill our souls. Oh, what a savior.

APPLICATION: If you are going through sorrow and sadness, realize that your solution is Jesus Christ. As it says in the Bible, "Christ is the only answer." Turn everything over to Him from this moment forward.

WEEK 37—THURSDAY

Little Nicks

SCRIPTURE READING: Colossians 6:16–26
THREE KEY WORDS: Nicks—Nature—Nurture

I. Nicks
Each day, as we go into the real world, we will face temptation. It is all around us—billboard advertising, magazines in the grocery stores, a friendly conversation with someone at work—and suddenly Satan will let little nicks of sinful thought enter our minds. Then, pretty soon we can let that little nick of sinful thought turn into one little nick of sinful action, by justifying our desire to do so. The problem is that nicks of sin will turn into numerous problems and eventually disaster.

II. Nature
Paul says in today's scripture that this is our nature. It is our nature to want to give into evil desires. He says it is a constant battle of the flesh against the spirit. This will produce nicks of sinful thought and then sinful action and as a result he says we cannot enter the Kingdom of God.

III. Nurture
Paul says to overcome this we must constantly nurture our relationship with the Holy Spirit. We must let Him control our lives and the results will be love, joy, peace, patience, kindness, and self-control. Don't let nature rule over you and cause you nicks of sin and unhappiness; instead nurture your friend the Holy Spirit.

APPLICATION: There is an old saying that says, "Don't expect God to help you overcome temptation if you continue to walk in the way of temptation." If you are fighting a battle with nature right now, release it to the Holy Spirit and let Him take control. Then find an accountability partner to help you with this battle. If you do, the fruit of the Spirit will come alive in you.

WEEK 37—FRIDAY

Pity or Rejoicing—Which Do You Choose?

SCRIPTURE READING: Philippians 4:1–8
THREE KEY WORDS: Trials—Temperament—Teachings

I. Trials
All of us, as we go through life, are going to face some trials and tribulation. We might face trials just because of our faith and what we believe; we will also face trials in sickness, loneliness, relationships, finances, family. When we face these trials the question is, will we be grateful or grumpy?

II. Temperament
When trials come into our lives, we will either *respond* or *react, rejoice* or *rebel*, be *grateful* or a *grouch*, be *humble* or *haughty*—it all comes down to temperament. There are no hopeless situations. We only lose hope in certain situations so it is our attitude or temperament toward trials that can make them a blessing or a burden.

III. Teachings
In John 5:11 Jesus taught, "That these things I have spoken to you that my joy may remain in you and that your joy may be full." In our scripture today, Paul says, "Rejoice in the Lord always," and again I say rejoice. Fix your thoughts on all the great things in life and not the bad. Remember, when trials come, have a spirit-filled temperament and rejoice in the Lord instead of having a pity party.

APPLICATION: As you start this day, if you are going through a trial, ask God to give you strength. Also follow the teachings in Paul's scriptures today and adjust your attitude toward rejoicing instead of regretting. Repent from your bad attitude and God will reward you.

WEEK 38—MONDAY
Helping Others

SCRIPTURE READING: Psalm 41
THREE KEY WORDS: Others—Ourselves—Obedience

I. Others

Jesus said that we are blessed when we help the poor. If you look at the life of Jesus, He always set self aside and served others. He ministered to the down and out. In fact, I have a plaque on my wall given to me by a friend that simply says "others." Lord, let this be my motto. Be that I might live for others and more like Jesus.

II. Ourselves

In today's word it is all about ourselves. I am too busy, my job must come first, I love my hobbies and need to participate in them on the weekends. I hardly have time for myself or family to worry about others. Nobody was busier than Jesus, but He always found time for others.

III. Obedience

Jesus said obedience is better than sacrifice, but in this case, we need to sacrifice to be obedient. Jesus said love your neighbor as yourself. Our ministry is to help the widows and orphans. That means putting self aside and serving others. Follow the example of our savior and be an other's person.

APPLICATION: As you pray today, ask the Lord to show you what areas of your life are keeping you from helping others. Take a personal inventory of your time, and then make a commitment that you are going to find one hour each week to help others.

WEEK 38—TUESDAY

Gate Closing

SCRIPTURE READING: Isaiah 51:1–10
THREE KEY WORDS: Grazing—Guilt—Gates

I. Grazing
Sometimes in our lives we are like animals grazing in the pasture. We might be feeding on the flesh and sin, or we might be feeding on the fruits of the spirit and walking with Christ. If we are grazing on sin, that is like eating chaffs of wheat, but if we are grazing on the spirit, then we will have a delicious green pasture. So what are we feeding our minds?

II. Guilt
If we are *grazing* on sin, but know we should be grazing on God, then that is going to produce guilt. Guilt is a disease that can eat like cancer; however, guilt can also be good because it provides our solutions. In order to get rid of guilt, we must confess our sins and get back to the green pastures of God.

III. Gates
Just like we must keep the gate closed to the pasture, so we must also close the gate on our past. Christ paid the price of our grazing in the pasture of sin so we could enjoy the green pastures of the future. Close the gate today and walk through the green pastures with the Holy Spirit.

APPLICATION: If you are grazing on sin today, (1 John 1:9) "Confess it and He will be faithful and just to forgive you." Get rid of the guilt also. Next, close the gate on bad thoughts and ask God to protect your mind and open your heart's gate to God's Word and feed on the fruit from doing so.

WEEK 38—WEDNESDAY

The Greatest Servants

SCRIPTURE READING: Judges 6:11–16
THREE KEY WORDS: Servants—Self—Success

I. Servants

Sometimes people put themselves down by saying, I am just a janitor or a housewife. I am only an average person. I happen to think that the janitor's job is quite important. Take all of the janitors out of the world and see how dirty everything would get. It is the same way in servanthood. Some of the greatest servants like Jesus are common people. In today's scripture, God chose a common man to fight a uncommon battle, and the common man won.

II. Self

When we let the flesh get in the way, we can't let God use us. We try to conquer our own battles in the flesh, and we lose out to Satan. When we can set self aside and let the savior take over, then we realize that no battle is too big. We must yield.

III. Success

When you look at all of the successful leaders in the Bible, they all put self second and God first. God was their source of power and wisdom. To be a servant, set *self aside* and *surrender to the Savior* and have a *servant's spirit*. We can have anything in life we want if we just help enough other people get what they want.

APPLICATION: God created everyone for a purpose. I don't care what position you hold in life, if you set self aside and surrender to the Savior, He will give you a servant's spirit and use you greatly. As you pray today, surrender yourself completely to God and let Him use you.

WEEK 38—THURSDAY

Jesus Wins

SCRIPTURE READING: Luke 11:14–23
THREE KEY WORDS: Demons—Devil—Deliverance

I. Demons
There definitely is a demonic spirit in the world. Jesus talked a lot about demons in the Bible. In fact, part of His ministry was to cast out demons. That is still true today. People can be demon-possessed because of witchcraft, astrology, or a number of cults and religions, but Jesus can still cast out the demons.

II. Devil
The devil is still in charge of the demons in his world, but he is not in charge of our will as Christians. The Bible says the devil is walking around like a roaring lion seeking whom he may devour, but we can beat him at his own game.

III. Deliverance
We were delivered from the demons and the devil when Jesus died on the cross and rose again. Jesus triumphed over Satan and sealed his doom. As it said today in the scripture, "Greater is He that is in you than he that is in the world." So beat up on Satan today.

APPLICATION: When the devil gets after you and you can sense the demons attacking you, claim the promise that greater is He that is in you than he that is in the world. Next, speak to the devil in a bold manner and say, "Get thee behind me, Satan. I claim victory over you in the name of Jesus." Then thank God for your victory.

WEEK 38—FRIDAY

Joy and Happiness

SCRIPTURE READING: Colossians 2:8–14
THREE KEY WORDS: Intelligence—Infinite—Imitation

I. Intelligence

We as people sometimes try to use our intelligence to find joy and happiness. It might be through studies in school, projects at work, studying different religions, the universe, or even evolution versus creation. We think our IQ will bring us contentment. It might challenge us, but will it give us peace?

II. Infinite

Our infinite God commands us to seek a relationship with Him—to love God with all our hearts—to love our neighbors as ourselves—to surrender our IQ—our intelligence. Surrender also our EQ—our emotional intelligence, along with our heart to Him completely. Then and only then will we feel happiness and joy.

III. Imitation

The smartest man who ever lived, Solomon, tried it all and when he was done he realized it came down to seeking the reverence of God. Fear God and keep His commandments. Jesus himself found joy and happiness in the simple things of life—loving and serving others. If you want joy and happiness, be an imitator of Christ.

APPLICATION: As you pray today, ask God to help you surrender your IQ, your EQ, and your heart to His will and way for your life. When you walk in God's will and let Him use the abilities He has given you, then the peace that passeth all understanding will give you joy and happiness.

WEEK 39—MONDAY

The Ministry of Grandparents

SCRIPTURE READING: Titus 2:1–5
THREE KEY WORDS: History—Heritage—Honor

I. History
Historically, grandparents have played an important part in the development of their grandchildren. If you study business, government, religion, and also the Bible, you will see the history and impact grandparents had in developing these areas. Many strong leaders attribute their success to their grandparents.

II. Heritage
The greatest heritage we can leave is a legacy of faith, godliness, gentleness, kindness, and love for family to our grandchildren to pass on from generation to generation. It is not the material things that will be remembered, but the moments we had together. Loving and leading them will be their greatest memory of us.

III. Honor
We as children and grandchildren should honor and respect our grandparents. The generation gap sometimes gets in our way. Grandparents can have greater impact on our children than we have because they have lived through everything the child and grandchild will live through. They already have the wisdom and knowledge as grandparents to show us how to keep from making some bad choices in our lives and prevent some real sorrow from taking place in our lives. The best lessons in life are learned through the mistakes of others.

APPLICATION: If you are fortunate enough to have living grandparents in your family, make them feel loved and appreciated by simply asking them for advice when you need it. They will be glad you did and you will be much better off for having done so.

WEEK 39—TUESDAY

Name Above All Names

SCRIPTURE READING: Philippians 2:1–21
THREE KEY WORDS: Influential—Impact—Invitation

I. Influential
As we look through history, there have been a lot of influential people who have made a contribution to our world. In politics, think of George Washington, Abraham Lincoln, John F. Kennedy, and Ronald Reagan. In sports think of Michael Jordan, Tiger Woods, and Muhammed Ali. In business, think of the Walton family, Lee Ioccoca, and Bill Gates. All of these people were influential, but the most influential name in history is Jesus. He changed our world more than all the others combined.

II. Impact
Although these names might have made an impact on our world, it was only for a period of history, but Jesus impacted the world from the very beginning through eternity. For the Christians, He impacted and changed our whole lives. Even though He died on the cross, He lives today and still impacts our world.

III. Invitation
If you would invite influential people to your home for dinner, they no doubt would make an impression or an impact, but when they left, it would all be over. But, with Jesus, you cannot only invite Him to your home, but you can be His home by inviting Him to live in your heart through the Holy Spirit. Do so today and it will impact you forever.

APPLICATION: Jesus loved the common person. The best way we can influence and impact people on a daily basis is to invite someone you know to let Jesus live in their heart as well. As you pray today, ask God to bring that opportunity into your life today, and also ask for the courage to do so.

WEEK 39—WEDNESDAY

Mistakes or Mistreated

SCRIPTURE READING: Romans 12:14–23
THREE KEY WORDS: Concern—Compassion—Christlike

I. Concern

In life, we all face mistakes and mistreatment. A mistake could cost us our job, or even break up a relationship. We might get mistreated by being overlooked for a position, or mistreated and abused by our family or friends. When this happens, it brings real concern into our lives about people and fairness.

II. Compassion

When this happens, we can let different emotions control us—anger, outrage, vengeance—but in today's scripture it says we are to show compassion. Don't pay back evil with evil. If someone is sad, share their sorrow and pray for them. Feed your enemy if necessary. When we do this others may be so overwhelmed, they will feel guilty. Show *compassion, concern,* but not *criticism.*

III. Christlike

Christ had every reason to be angry and outraged when His disciples deserted Him while soldiers beat Him and hung Him on the cross. Instead Christ showed love, compassion, and concern when He said, "Father, forgive them, they know not what they do." He also showed compassion to the disciples when He saw them after the resurrection. We need to do the same as well. This is *concern* and *compassion* for others.

APPLICATION: No doubt, there is someone in your past or present who has hurt you deeply. You also may know someone you have hurt as well. In either case, do what Christ did and forgive them. That is the Christlike way of making it right.

WEEK 39—THURSDAY

Life's Tribulations

SCRIPTURE READING: Romans 5:1–5
THREE KEY WORDS: Persecution—Persevere—Patience

I. **Persecution**
As we go through life, we are going to face persecution. It might be because of the stand we take at work, in the community, or even with our own family. In today's scripture, Paul is persecuted for taking a stand. We sometimes cannot avoid it, but we can handle it if we understand that God is building character through it.

II. **Persevere**
No matter how tough our persecution or tribulations might be, we must persevere and hang in there. It is a daily thing. Yesterday is a canceled check, tomorrow is a promissory note, so this day is the first day of the rest of our lives. Therefore, persevere daily. It might be painful but with God's help and our attitude, it can also be pleasurable in the end.

III. **Patience**
Patience is a virtue that is very hard for some people to develop. God give me patience, but "hurry" is sometimes our prayer. The reason we suffer persecution or tribulation is because God uses both of these to develop our patience. We need to remain *steadfast*, *strong*, and *surrender* to God's will when we suffer persecution or tribulation in our lives.

APPLICATION: If you are going through persecution right now, ask God to give you the perseverance and patience to make it through. The light you see at the end of the tunnel is the light of Jesus waiting to help you through. Surrender it all to Him today.

WEEK 39—FRIDAY

Business' Greatest Asset

SCRIPTURE READING: Colossians 3:22–41
THREE KEY WORDS: People—Principle—Perfect

I. People

There is an old saying that people are our greatest asset, but most of the time we treat it only as a saying. My friend Zig Ziglar says you can get everything in life you want if you will help enough other people get what they want. In business and in life that has to be a philosophy, not a tactic. If it is a tactic, it is wrong. If it is a philosophy, it is biblical.

II. Principle

In today's scripture, Paul shows us how it is a principle. As bosses, we are to give our best and be just and fair with our employees. Why? Because God should be our partner in all we do, not just business. Lou Holtz once said, "Do right, do your best, and treat others like they want to be treated." Our master in Heaven expects our best.

III. Perfect

Many years ago in the 1970s, when I had six retail stores, God gave me this saying: when *policies, procedures, programs,* and *products* become more important than *people,* we've got a *problem.* It is really the golden rule that counts in life, so let's put it into practice every day.

APPLICATION: In your busy world today, practice the principle of the golden rule. It is a biblical principle that we should strive for daily. It is also the best evangelistic tool for letting people see Christ in us. Make that commitment as you start your day.

WEEK 40—MONDAY
Standards

SCRIPTURE READING: Isaiah 6:1–10
THREE KEY WORDS: Standards—Sight—Sin

I. Standards

God has standards that we must live by. These standards are important to Him, and also important to our relationship with Him. It is also our testimony to others. Unfortunately, today in the church, as well as personally, we see in many cases that we have let our standards slip and I believe it is grieving God.

II. Sight

Are we trying to measure our standards to the world's view or God's sight? We can compromise God's standards to come down to the world's standards or we can take a stand and be what God wants us to be. That is why God says we must go into all the world to reach people, but we are not to become a part of their world to do so.

III. Sin

When we compromise God's standards, we commit sin. All have sinned and come short of the glory of God. In God's sight, we are sinners or saints. We can't live the perfect life but God says obedience is better than sacrifice. Be strong on standards and keep your sight on God.

APPLICATION: As you pray today, ask God to reveal an area of your life where you have lowered your standards. It might be music, dress, entertainment, or the people we run with. Ask Him also for the desire and power to have godly standards in your everyday living. It will make you a better witness for Him.

WEEK 40—TUESDAY

I *Need* Hope

SCRIPTURE READING: Lamentations Chapter 3
THREE KEY WORDS: Heart—Hope—Help

I. Heart
Sometimes life gets so heavy that my heart feels like it could explode. Circumstances or tragedies come into our lives that break our hearts. We sometimes get up each day and say, "If only I can make it through another day. My strength is gone. My heart is so heavy."

II. Hope
When this happens we can lose hope, but because of Jesus and what He has done for us, we always have hope. In fact, the good old hymnal says, "My hope is found on nothing less than Jesus Christ and righteousness." He is our one hope to heal a heavy heart.

III. Help
When we have a heavy heart and feel hopeless, God's help is just a prayer away. The word says His compassion fails not—it is new every morning. God is always faithful to help us. Each day as I start, I say, "Father, I need your help. I am heavy and burdened. Please help me." Then I am reminded to "Cast all your cares on Him because He cares for you."

APPLICATION: If you are dealing with a heavy heart today, don't lose hope. Ask God for help and He will give you the help you need. Surrender it all to Him and let Him carry the burden for you. Then, thank Him for doing so.

WEEK 40—WEDNESDAY
Developing Others

SCRIPTURE READING: 2 Timothy 2:1–5
THREE KEY WORDS: Mentoring—Molding—Maturing

I. Mentoring

In today's scripture, Paul is telling Timothy to teach others as He taught him. As Christians, we are to mentor others by winning and mentoring them. When you think back on your life, if you had a mentor, that person really impacted you. If not, we all could have kept from making a lot of mistakes in our lives if we had someone teaching us basic biblical principles.

II. Molding

In the mentoring process, we are molding people's character as well as developing their knowledge. Like the hymn says, "Mold me and make me after thy will, while I am waiting yielded and still." We mold others. We need to ask God to help us and to develop others according to His will, not what we want them to do or become.

III. Maturing

Mentoring and *molding* develops *maturity*. If we take in a young business person, we are mentoring them to become mature in business. The same is true in spiritual maturity. They are babes in Christ and we are developing their *maturity* so they can *mentor*, *mold*, and *mature* someone as well.

APPLICATION: There is an old saying that says, "He or she who teaches, learns twice." That is what mentoring is all about. If you are not mentoring someone, find a young person or a new believer and commit to that person's development through the mentoring process. It will be a highlight you will never forget.

WEEK 40—THURSDAY
Take Responsibility for Sin

SCRIPTURE READING: Ezekiel 18:1–18
THREE KEY WORDS: Evil—Excuses—Example

I. Evil
In today's world we see a lot of evil. It is hard to understand why people commit such evil like a mother drowning five of her kids in a bathtub, a preacher executed for killing an abortion doctor and his assistant, a husband who leaves his wife and kids to run off with another woman. Evil in business, war, and society. Satan is seeking whom he may kill and destroy.

II. Excuses
In a great number of these situations, these people make excuses for what they did. The preacher says, "God told Him to do it so he will be rewarded in Heaven." The husband says, "I don't love you anymore. It is all about me. I want my happiness. Life is short and I want all the gusto I can get." In today's scripture, God says it is my rule that man should die for his sins. No excuses, you are responsible.

III. Example
Jesus is our example for today's responsibilities, though. He didn't deserve to die on the cross, He knew the Father sent Him for this purpose. When we sin, don't make excuses, just take responsibility and ask Jesus to forgive you. This also sets an example for others.

APPLICATION: No matter where we are or what we are doing, we can't allow evil to overcome us or make excuses for doing so. Today and every day, be an example to others by taking a stand against evil and being a living example.

WEEK 40—FRIDAY
Simply Grace

SCRIPTURE READING: 1 Peter 5
THREE KEY WORDS: Grace—Gift—Guidance

I. Grace
There are some things in life that are hard for me to understand and accept. One of these is the grace of God. I get so busy that I don't even feel spiritual, let alone act spiritual. There are times that I know I commit willful sin because of the pressure I am under. I don't feel worthy and I feel like I need to work my way back to God. What happens when we feel this way?

II. Gift
Remember that because of what Christ did for us on the cross that we need to repent, and through the grace of God, ask forgiveness and be restored. We can't earn God's grace. In fact, Ephesians 2:8-9 says we are saved by grace, not works, so if we can be saved by grace, we can also be restored by grace. What a great gift from God.

III. Guidance
In today's scripture, God's goodness is shown by being humble. He gives grace to the humble. He also wants us to do the same for others. The same grace that is available to us through God, we should also show to others each day. Be kind and gentle and not judgmental. Put others first as Christ did.

APPLICATION: As you pray today, thank God for His wonderful gift of grace, then ask Him for guidance in every area of your life as you go out to serve and be a witness for Him. We need grace and guidance daily.

WEEK 41—MONDAY
Don't Worry—God Hears Us
(THE HOLY SPIRIT INTERCEDES)

SCRIPTURE READING: Romans 8:26–27
THREE KEY WORDS: Hard—Heart—Hear

I. Hard

Sometimes when I kneel to pray early in the morning, I have such a hard time. My mind is wandering; I am thinking about a busy day. I don't feel good, and frankly I sometimes ask myself, "Is He hearing me?" I have prayed for certain things and certain people everyday for thirty years, and if I am not careful, I become like a robot just praying.

II. Heart

As I feel this way, I think how the Bible says that man looks upon the outer appearance, but God looks upon the heart. He doesn't care if I am standing up, laying down, driving in my car, or just whispering under my breath. God hears my heart. He knows that no matter how often or how many times I have prayed for something or someone that my heart is sincere.

III. Hear

God also hears the prayers of the righteous. If our hearts are right, and we are in fellowship with God, He hears and He answers. Sometimes it is so hard, but don't worry, because in today's scripture it says that the Holy Spirit knows what we need and He is praying for us. So when it is hard, remember we have the Spirit praying for us and God will always listen.

APPLICATION: One of the things I have tried to do in my relationship and walk with the Lord is simply to have conversational prayer with the Father. He is always there listening, so if a need comes to your mind or heart, just explain it to God in an easy, simple way. He will hear and the Holy Spirit will also help you.

WEEK 41—TUESDAY
Words Don't Work

SCRIPTURE READING: Romans 3:21–28
THREE KEY WORDS: Needs—Nice—New

I. Needs
As we live our lives daily, we all have needs to be met. They might be physical, mental, spiritual, or even financial. It might even be that we just need someone to talk to. We need to be sensitive to the needs of others, and to show them their greatest need of all, and that is the need for Christ. He can help meet all the needs in this life.

II. Nice
It is good to be nice to people. As Christians, we should strive to do so, but the facts are that it takes more than being nice to make it to heaven. A great number of really nice people who do good works by helping others or giving a lot of money to the church, have not made it to heaven. Why? Because their niceness got in the way of their seeing their need for Christ.

III. New
The Bible says that now is the day of salvation, tomorrow might be too late. So as we go out today, let's be nice to people. Also be sensitive to their needs, but let's also take the time to point them to the cross so they can see Jesus and be in heaven some day.

APPLICATION: Think of someone you know who has a real need today. Be nice to them with a simple call or visit. Ask them how you can help. Have a listening ear. Be sure to pray with them and point them to the cross where Christ can meet their every need.

WEEK 41—WEDNESDAY

Complaining to God

SCRIPTURE READING: Exodus 7:1–7
THREE KEY WORDS: Complaining—Concern—Consider

I. Complaining

When things don't always go our way, or we think that God is not hearing our prayers or caring about us, the first thing we want to do is complain. That can be a dangerous thing. In today's scripture it says they tested God by complaining. We must remember that God has a plan for us, and all things work together for our good, even when we don't think so.

II. Concern

When you get in the spirit of complaining, we should be concerned about our hearts. Are we in tune with God's Spirit through our spirit? The devil wants us to complain because that is of the flesh, but if we walk in the spirit, our complaints will go away and our concerns will be to become Christ-like.

III. Consider

When we get grumpy and complain, just consider where you were before Christ came into your life. As the Christian song says, "When I think of where He brought me from to where I am today, that is the reason why I love Him so." When you consider all of the wonderful blessings from God, your complaints will go away.

APPLICATION: If you are concerned about your bad attitude or complaining, stop and consider all God has done for you today. Take a piece of paper and spend ten minutes listing all of God's blessings. Thank Him, and I guarantee your attitude will change to gratitude.

WEEK 41—THURSDAY
The Freedom of Knowing Truth

SCRIPTURE READING: John 8:28–36
THREE KEY WORDS: Truth—Trust—Tell

I. Truth
There is only one truth, and that is the Word of God. Like it says in today's scripture, "Ye shall know the truth and the truth shall set you free." People search all over for the truth, but what they are really looking for is the gray area of truth, so they can do what they want. It is very simple. The truth of the Word is simply black and white, whether we like it or not.

II. Trust
Once we have learned the truth and live with the truth in us, then we must trust God in everything we do. We must have faith and trust Romans 8:28 that all things work together for good. Also when we die, we are absent from the body and present with the Lord. That is truth to trust God for everything.

III. Tell
God always wants us to tell the truth no matter what, but also He wants us to tell others about the truth of the Gospel. It is our responsibility to go into all the world and tell others about the truth of Jesus Christ, that He died on the cross for our sins, was buried and arose the third day, and will come back to earth again to take us to heaven.

APPLICATION: If you have doubts about truth, make a commitment today that you believe that God's Word is 100 percent true. Trust God to build that confidence in you, then call someone you know about the truth of the gospel. It will be a great day for you both.

WEEK 41—FRIDAY

Why Repent?

SCRIPTURE READING: Psalm 51
THREE KEY WORDS: Repenting—Rejoicing—Revelation

I. Repenting
Repenting isn't always fun, but it is necessary. We can't continue to live in willful sin and have the joy of our salvation or fellowship with God. I have always said that an unsaved person is happier than a backslider. Why? Because they have never had the joy or peace of salvation.

II. Rejoicing
As David said in today's scripture, "Restore unto me the joy of my salvation." There is nothing more joyful than the day we are saved. Just think back to that moment in your life and what a wonderful experience salvation was—burdens lifted, peace and joy in your heart, and the joy of telling others about Christ. What a joy.

III. Revelation
When David said, "Father, restore unto me the joy of my salvation." You can look at David and see just how miserable he was, just like some of us. Just as Jesus died for salvation, He also died for restoration and the joy we receive. The decision is ours, sin and suffering, or restoration and joyfulness.

APPLICATION: If you are miserable right now because of sin in your life or a hard heart, do as David did. Repent and ask God to give back to you the joy you once had. He will restore you and the angels in heaven will rejoice, as will the people who love you. Don't delay, do it today.

WEEK 42—MONDAY

How Secure Are We?

SCRIPTURE READING: Ephesians 1–6
THREE KEY WORDS: Safe—Secure—Shields

I. Safe

As I write this, we are remembering the second anniversary of 9/11/2001 when our country's safety was shattered. Today it is so much different than before. When traveling by airplane, we have to allow more time. As I step onto a plane, a brief thought of fear might go through my mind. Am I really safe?

II. Secure

Nothing ever guarantees our safety or security while we are here on earth, but God has promised those who are born again that we are *safe* and *secure* in the arms of our *Savior*. God the Father says that we are sealed until the day of redemption, and that no one can break that seal. We are safe and secure until that time. That does not guarantee us safety here on earth, but it promised security for our future and all eternity.

III. Shields

Just like we see more types of protection on earth to prevent another 9/11, we must have shields in our spiritual lives as well. In fact, God says to daily put on our shields, the whole armor of God to protect us from the evil one. We are safe and secure, but Satan is still out there, so wear your shield daily and take with you the sword of the Spirit, God's Word.

APPLICATION: As the old hymn says, "We are safe and secure in the arms of Jesus." The only real security we have is eternal security. Take your shield of faith with you today and feel the secure, safe presence of God with you wherever you go.

WEEK 42—TUESDAY

Is It Really Worth It?

SCRIPTURE READING: 2 Corinthians 4:1–10
THREE KEY WORDS: Weary—Worry—Wholly

I. Weary

As we get older and look back on our lives, sometimes we say, "Have I really made a difference?" We get really tired and weary. I have been doing the same thing day after day and I am really weary. Sometimes I don't think I can make it, but then God shows me one life that I touched and made a difference in, and I gather the strength to go on.

II. Worry

From weariness, sometimes comes worry. We start thinking about our future and can I slow down a little? Am I going to be okay financially, or is my health going to be good? We also get concerned about our families and loved ones, but God says when we are tired, to wait upon Him and He will renew our strength. When we worry, we are to cast all our cares upon Him because He cares for us. We just need to trust and do it.

III. Wholly

When we face weariness and we worry, God says, "Give me yourself wholly." In other words, trust in the Lord with all your heart and lean not unto your own understanding. Don't worry, don't weary, just be wholly committed to trust God.

APPLICATION: If you are tired and weary, and are also worrying about something, as you pray today, meditate on the scripture, give yourself wholly to God. Surrender it all to Him and He will handle it for you.

WEEK 42—WEDNESDAY

The Blessing of Giving

SCRIPTURE READING: Acts 20:33–38
THREE KEY WORDS: Getting—Giving—Going

I. Getting
There is a phrase that says, "Get all the gusto in life you can. You only go around once." We spend so much time working hard just to get things we don't really need. I think of people who just want to *get* no matter the cost. They get in the bondage of getting things: recognition, promotions, acceptance, and live their lives in chaos.

II. Giving
The Bible says it is more blessed to give than to receive. Giving not only to the Kingdom for blessings, but also giving to those in need is such a rich reward. Why do people have garage sales? Because the accumulating results in too much. Instead of selling it, give it, and God will reward you for doing so.

III. Going
Our giving is a ministry for us. God also tells us to go and seek others. One of the ways to do this is giving of ourselves to others in community work, church work, or visiting the sick. For the Christian, getting all the gusto we can in life is found in giving and going for our Father.

APPLICATION: If you are working hard to get everything in life, make a commitment today that you are going to spend the next day giving and going—giving of your time, money, and talents. As the scripture says today, it is more blessed to give than receive. Be a giver today.

WEEK 42—THURSDAY

Winning the Battle of Trials

SCRIPTURE READING: James 1:2–12
THREE KEY WORDS: Testings—Tribulation—Triumphant

I. Testings
Every day we will face some kind of test. I didn't like tests in school and I still don't like tests, but they are a part of life. There are many tests—some are temptations to do wrong. We might face a test of our integrity at work, or a test with a friend or family member. The question is, will you yield or pass the test?

II. Tribulation
Some of our tests can turn into real tribulation. We might yield to sin and face disaster, yield at work or lose our job, lose a friendship or we might face the tribulation of finances or a severe illness. It is a fact that we are going to face *trials*, *tribulations* and *tests*, but there is victory for the believer.

III. Triumphant
God says I can do all things through Christ. There is no test, trial, or tribulation that He would allow to come into our lives that we can't bear. The next time you face a test, before it turns into tribulation, look to Jesus because He is the answer.

APPLICATION: When we are tested and tried, remember the triumphant victory of Christ in the resurrection. When He left, He said He would give us another comforter, the Holy Spirit. Today in your testing or tribulation, ask the Holy Spirit for power and comfort to win the battle. Together you can be triumphant.

WEEK 42—FRIDAY

Listen—God Is Talking

SCRIPTURE READING: Colossians 3:10–12
THREE KEY WORDS: Silence—Savior—Sermon

I. Silence

We get so busy in our everyday world that sometimes we just need to sit still, listen for God, and listen to God. That is what the word meditate means. When you finish reading a scripture or a devotion, sit for five minutes, close your eyes, tune your ears and listen. God will speak to your spirit about what you need, and also what you need to pray for. We need to listen.

II. Savior

The Bible says that on many occasions Jesus went out on His own to pray. He got away by Himself, prayed to the Father, and then He listened to what the Father wanted Him to do. If God's only begotten Son thought it important enough to be silent and listen, shouldn't we, His adopted sons and daughters, do the same?

III. Sermon

Silence is golden, as the old saying goes, and sometimes it can be the best sermon we hear. God will use a scripture, a devotion, a circumstance or a person that comes into our mind or spirit as we meditate, and the Holy Spirit Himself will tell us what it means or what we need to do. When God speaks, He is the best preacher of all and will give you a great sermon, so stop and listen to what God has to say today.

APPLICATION: As you pray today, set aside some extra time to be silent. Ask God to give you a mini-sermon for your heart and to speak to your spirit. If you tune everything out and tune Him in, you will hear from God. He is listening and will reply. Be ready for His answer by listening as well.

WEEK 43—MONDAY

The Blessing of Serving

SCRIPTURE READING: Ruth 1
THREE KEY WORDS: Serve—Support—Sacrifice

I. Serve

When our Savior walked the earth, He served others. Even though He was the King of Kings and Lord of Lords, He found true meaning and joy in serving others. He wants us to do the same. To serve is to love. People have a lot of needs and hurts and a simple thing like a visit, or a phone call can mean so much to someone. We need to take time to do so.

II. Support

Another way we can serve is to support others. It may be that we can serve them financially or it may be by supporting them with prayer. I think the greatest support we can give someone is just to take time to show we care, and to love them and support them as the best friends we can be. *Look, listen,* and *love* is a great way to support.

III. Sacrifice

I know that to serve and support someone can be inconvenient and take a lot of time. It is no doubt a sacrifice. Don't forget that God served us and supported us by sacrificing His most precious gift, His only begotten Son. If God can sacrifice like that, we can sacrifice in care and support for others.

APPLICATION: Think of someone you know today who needs your support. It could be prayer support, financial support, or doing something special for that person. Then, make a sacrifice of time or dollars to serve that person by supporting him or her. That is what God did for us, so we should do it as well.

WEEK 43—TUESDAY

We Are Sojourners

SCRIPTURE READING: Colossians 1
THREE KEY PHRASES: The Tunnel—The Triumph—The Transition

I. The Tunnel

Sometimes life is like living in a tunnel, where things get dark and dreary. Problems overwhelm us and there seems no way out. Sin might make our tunnels even darker. When we live in willful sin, Satan's darkness is horrible. This is what can cause life to be dark for us, but suddenly, through the Holy Spirit, we can see a light at the end of the tunnel and it is not a train going the wrong way. It is Jesus with His arms wide open waiting to help us.

II. The Triumph

Through Jesus and what He did on the cross, we can have victory over Satan and the darkness of life. The bright light of Jesus now shines in our hearts. That doesn't mean we still won't experience times of darkness, but it does mean that the light of hope and love through Christ is always there to help us.

III. The Transition

Some day we will transition from the *tunnel of life* on earth to the *tranquillity of joy* and peace in heaven, where there is no darkness, but only pure beautiful light that we can enjoy for all eternity. If you are in the tunnel today, look to Jesus for your triumph.

APPLICATION: There is nothing worse than being in total darkness. It is a frightening experience. If you feel like you are in the tunnel of darkness today, or if you are in the darkness of willful sin, turn to the Light of the World, Jesus. Confess your sin, repent, and He will immediately brighten your world and walk with you side by side. Then, look forward to the transition to heaven.

WEEK 43—WEDNESDAY

Where Can God Use Me?

SCRIPTURE READING: 1 Timothy 6:15–19
THREE KEY WORDS: Anywhere—Anytime—Available

I. Anywhere

God can use us anywhere we want to be used. The key is, do we want to? He can use me in the office, at church, visiting a neighbor, the butcher, the baker, or the candlestick maker. We can all be used anywhere we go if we will take the time and effort to do so.

II. Anytime

God can also use us anytime he pleases. It might be every day, once a week, or anytime He chooses to bring someone into my path to be a witness to, or to help others. There are people all around us daily who are ready to minister to if we just make ourselves available at anytime to the leading of the Spirit of God.

III. Available

Every day we just need to say, God, I am available. How do you want to use me today? Where do you want me to go? When should I go and what should I do? When we make ourselves available and surrender to Him, God will use us *anywhere, anytime* and *any place* and we will be blessed beyond our imagination.

APPLICATION: As you pray today, tell the Lord that you are available to be used by Him anywhere or anytime He chooses. Ask Him to bring someone into your life today that you can minister to. Then be sensitive to the leading of the Holy Spirit as you go through the day so you can be ready when God calls.

WEEK 43—THURSDAY
Life Is Relevant

SCRIPTURE READING: Psalm 19:1–11
THREE KEY WORDS: Relevant—Revelation—Riches

I. Relevant
Throughout history, the one thing that never changes is God's Word. Cultures might change, but as the Bible says, "Jesus is the same yesterday, today and forever." That is the same with God's Word. It will last forever. Everything in this world will pass away, but God's Word is relevant for the past, present, and future.

II. Revelation
God reveals everything in life we need to know if we will only study it. He tells us how to raise our children, how to build a better marriage, run a business, develop relationships, handle grief, deal with difficult people, and even reveals our future and where we will live forever. It is the miracle of life. It is our choice to receive it or reject it.

III. Riches
God's Word contains all of the riches in life as well. In fact it says that Jesus came to give us life abundant. It shows us how to enjoy all of God's wonderful blessings and the riches of the simple things in life. If things seem tough, read God's Word for comfort. It is relevant, gives revelation, and is full of riches.

APPLICATION: There is nothing you face in life today that does not have an answer in the Bible. It is relevant to our time and God will reveal what you need if you will make the effort to study His Word. When you do, you will also enjoy all of the blessings from it as well. Look to God's Word today.

WEEK 43—FRIDAY

Total Trust

SCRIPTURE READING: Psalm 89
THREE KEY WORDS: Taste—Test—Trust

I. Taste
Many times, as we go through life, we taste a lot of good things as well as experience great moments. We might taste a delicious new food or dessert. We also might taste the goodness of developing a new friendship, or sharing a wonderful memory with an old friend, but sometimes we taste the sour things of life as well. We face problems, sickness, or sadness. It is all part of life, but there is no better taste than being in the presence of almighty God. To feel His Spirit in our lives is so wonderful.

II. Test
When the taste of life turns sour and we face a real testing in our lives, we need to do two things. First, we need to remember that we have been tested before, and that God would not allow us to be tested any more than we can handle. Second, God has a purpose in our testing—to make us more like Christ.

III. Trust
We also must trust God for our blessings and testings. He has promised that He will never leave us or forsake us. So trust in Him with all your heart. Whether tasting the good or the bad, trust God. As the scripture says, "trust in the Lord with all your heart, and lean not unto your own understanding. In all your ways, acknowledge Him and He will direct your path."

APPLICATION: Take time today to taste the good things in life. Look at God's creations, and play a rerun in your mind of past blessings. If you are going through a time of testing, trust God to turn that test into a taste of victory and give it all to Him. This is the beginning of tasting the great things of life.

WEEK 44—MONDAY

God Is My Partner

SCRIPTURE READING: Matthew 6:5–15
THREE KEY WORDS: Partner—Prayer—Privilege

I. Partner

God is my partner in everything I do. When I pray, He is my partner. When I have problems, decisions to make, business to conduct, or children to raise God is there to be my partner if I will only let Him. He is always there, twenty-four hours a day, to be my partner. I need to realize that I don't need to do everything on my own. The greatest partner a person could have is God, and we always have Him with us.

II. Prayer

One of the greatest areas of partnership with God is prayer. Just like I used to sit down and get advice from my dad, I can sit down and get advice from my Heavenly Dad. Praying to God, my partner, is no different than talking to any other partner, whether my spouse or business partner. We have discussions with them and we can also have discussions with our partner—God Himself—anytime we want.

III. Privilege

We should thank God every day for the privilege of not only being His partner but also His child. Since we are His children, our partnership is even closer. Just remember our partnership is eternal and nothing is too big or small for my Father and partner.

APPLICATION: As you go through your day, remember your partner is with you through the Holy Spirit living in you. If you are facing problems, or have decisions to make, turn to your partner in prayer and discuss it with Him. Then, thank God for the privilege of doing so.

WEEK 44—TUESDAY

Riches in God's Word

SCRIPTURE READING: Psalm 119:1–16
THREE KEY WORDS: Treasure—Truth—Testimony

I. Treasure

God's Word is a real treasure that we should store in our hearts. People search for treasure sometimes in great detail and if they find one, they will store it away in a safe place. David said that God's Word is a real treasure. We must search it, read it, memorize it and live it. Seek it as treasure, because where your treasure is there, will your heart be also.

II. Truth

God's Word is also truth. The Bible says, "Ye shall know the truth and the truth shall set you free." God's Word is the only truth to live, make decisions, and to prepare for the future by. Philosophy and psychology can vary from person to person, but God's truth is the same for everyone.

III. Testimony

The more we know the truth of God's Word and store it in our hearts, the better testimony we can be, because we should be more like Jesus—more loving, kind, gentle, joyful, and pure. By doing so we can minister to people who are hurting. Treasure the truth of God's Word and be a testimony for Him.

APPLICATION: As a suggestion to know the treasure of God's Word and to develop truth in your life, I would challenge you for the next 31 days to read a chapter a day in Proverbs. It is a treasure full of truth, and it will help you to be a better testimony in every area of your life. Try it for 31 days and it will also be a blessing to you.

WEEK 44—WEDNESDAY

He Still Works

SCRIPTURE READING: Hebrews 7:23–28
THREE KEY WORDS: Our Problem—Our Priest—Our Provider

I. Our Problem

As I get older and look at the world in which we live, it seems like life is fulll of problems. They may be financial, health, family, relationships and any number of other things. Sometimes it seems like there is no hope. We see light at the end of the tunnel, but it looks like it is a train coming the wrong way. We say to ourselves, "what do we do?"

II. Our Priest

When Christ died for our sins on the cross and said "it is finished," that was really a new beginning for Him and for us. He arose three days later sitting at the right hand of our Father, and His new work began. That work is Him being our High Priest, taking all of our problems to the Father. It is also a new beginning for us because at His resurrection we were released from the law and live under grace and mercy. The High Priest is pleading for us constantly.

III. Our Provider

God the Father hears those pleas that our Priest is taking to Him. The Bible says that He answers all of our prayers. Sometimes it may not be what we want to hear, but He always answers. It is always better to get a hard 'no' than a soft 'maybe', but He also says 'yes' as well. He will only provide what is best for us.

APPLICATION: If you have a bucket-load of problems in your life right now and don't know what to do, take some time and get alone with God in a dark room. Tell our High Priest about them and He will hear your plea and take them to the Provider. Then sit still for ten to fifteen minutes and wait to hear His still, small voice. It will come if you listen.

WEEK 44—THURSDAY
Getting the Reward

SCRIPTURE READING: 1 Corinthians. 9:24–27
THREE KEY WORDS: Goals—Grit—God

I. Goals
Life has much more purpose and fulfillment when we have goals. The thing we must remember, however, is that our goals need to be in accordance with God's Word. Many people focus on materialism or personal achievement with goal-setting and can get their lives out of balance. When we set goals, we must do so in every area of life and then ask God to show us His will for reaching those goals.

II. Grit
To reach a goal takes a lot of grit and hard work. Paul says that here on earth if we grind and grit it out, we will win some temporary prizes. However, our daily grit and grind should be to work toward the prize of our eternal rewards in Heaven. This is our main goal.

III. God
Paul says that someday we will stand before God, and will receive our rewards for our faithfulness to Him and the goals we accomplished living for Him, as well as the ones we brought to Heaven. As we grind it out here and go for the gold, the greatest praise we can hear is: "well done, good and faithful servant."

APPLICATION: Life is tough, but when we are tough on ourselves, life becomes easier for us. Part of that is having and working toward some goals in our lives. Ask God to give you some meaningful eternal goals to work toward and then grit it out daily. God will help you and the rewards will be worth all of the hard work.

WEEK 44—FRIDAY
God's Glory

SCRIPTURE READING: Psalm 3
THREE KEY WORDS: Glory—Goodness—Grace

I. Glory
Significance can also be translated to God's glory. God's glory sometimes is thought of as beautiful and majestic, which it is, but it also means He is there to lift our burden and give us comfort in times of trouble or even tragedy. He is our shield, our glory, and He will hold us up when we can't hold up anymore.

II. Goodness
God is so good. Isn't it great to know that when someone else is against us, God's goodness always prevails. His goodness is there at all times when we need it. When we are down, just think about how good God has been to us and remember His glory.

III. Grace
It is only through the grace of God and Jesus dying on the cross for our sins that we can share in both God's glory and goodness. We should always be grateful that we don't have to earn it. If you are discouraged or depressed today, give God glory because of His goodness and grace, and He will lift you up.

APPLICATION: No matter what happens in our lives, we are to glorify God. This pleases Him more than anything. When we think of all His goodness and grace we are saved through faith, it should be easy for us to give God glory and also bring Him glory.

WEEK 45—MONDAY
The Importance of Words

SCRIPTURE READING: Proverbs 12
THREE KEY WORDS: Encouragement—Enlightenment—Enjoyment

I. Encouragement
Broken bones don't hurt as much as a broken spirit. I have had some broken bones in my life that have been painful, but they healed quickly. I have also had a heart broken from words spoken to me that were much more painful, and I am still in the healing process from them. Millions of people go to bed hungry for food, but many more go to bed looking for a kind word, or a word of encouragement. We need to feed people with encouragement.

II. Enlightenment
The Word of God is given to us to enlighten us as to how to live life and love others. In God's Word it says that we are to treat others like we want to be treated, and also to love our neighbors as we love ourselves. Those two short messages enlighten us about how to encourage others.

III. Enjoyment
When we encourage and enlighten others, it will bring real enjoyment to our hearts and souls. I heard someone say that if you feel discouraged or depressed, find someone who feels the same way, encourage that person, and your discouragement will go away. As we touch people today, give them a word of encouragement.

APPLICATION: As usual, today will be a busy day. The best way that we can enjoy this day is to give someone an encouraging word and we will enlighten his or her life by doing so.

WEEK 45—TUESDAY
Hurting People

SCRIPTURE READING: 2 Corinthians 2:1–4
THREE KEY WORDS: Compassion—Consolation—Comfort

I. Compassion

As we meet people every day, we don't realize that they can really be hurting. They might have recently lost a loved one, gone through a divorce, may have a serious illness, and are hurting. We need to learn how to show compassion to others who are hurting. Paul said we need compassion when we go through suffering so we can show it to others.

II. Consolation

One of the gifts that Jesus had and that we need to learn is how to console people when they are grieving. Grief is a terrible experience to go through and it is difficult to minister to a person who is grieving, but if we have compassion and can console them by being there when they need us, provide a listening ear, ane engage in a time of prayer—that is what is important. Compassion and consoling is simply time spent with them.

III. Comfort

Whether we are grieving or someone we know is, we can always find comfort in the Word of God. God's Word says His understanding is unlimited. He feels our pain and grief. He bore our sorrows, but sometimes we need each other as well. Find someone who is hurting. You don't have to look far, then show *compassion, consolation,* and *comfort.*

APPLICATION: Are you going through a tough time right now? If so, ask God to console and comfort you. He promises to do so in His Word. Also ask Him to show you someone you can comfort and console. In return, it will help to comfort and console you. This is real compassion.

WEEK 45—WEDNESDAY
God's Goodness

SCRIPTURE READING: Psalm 23
THREE KEY PHRASES: Goodness—Guidance—Grateful

I. Goodness
We occasionally need to take time to think of all the good things God has done for us. As the scripture says today, "His goodness and mercy shall follow me every day of my life." We might not think it is good, but all things work together for good. The fact that Jesus kept us out of hell should be good enough, even if nothing else good ever happens.

II. Guidance
God also guides us daily if we will only let Him. He guides me beside still waters. He guides my paths and the steps I take if I will surrender my will to His. He guides me in every decision I make, and every place I go. What better guide through life can I have than God Himself?

III. Grateful
We should be so grateful for all the things God has done and will do for us. We should take time as the song says, "Count your blessings one by one, count your blessings, see what God has done." We take our blessings for granted, but today, look at God's goodness. Seek His guidance and be forever grateful.

APPLICATION: In your prayer time today, meditate on all the good things God has done for you. Ask Him for guidance in everything you do, and at the end of the day, show your gratefulness by thanking and praising Him.

WEEK 45—THURSDAY

What Will I Leave Behind?

SCRIPTURE READING: John 10
THREE KEY WORDS: Epitaph—Effect—Example

I. Epitaph

Many times we worry about what people say about us while we are here on earth. We hear both the good and the bad, and if we are Christlike, we will try to make a good impression. The real question, however, is what will they say about us when we are gone? Did we show good character and were we Christlike in our daily walk? Did we display the fruits of the spirit?

II. Effect

Daily we should make a real effort to be Christlike so we can help others and show them the path to eternal life. The old saying that we might be the best Bible someone might read puts a heavy responsibility on us to live a godly life. We need to make that effort daily.

III. Example

The Bible says that as a child imitates his father, we should also imitate the qualities and characteristics of our Father and be an example. My sister lived only twenty-one years. Because of her effort and example in being Christlike and showing others the road to heaven, her epitaph on her tombstone, as I said in an earlier message, is 2 Timothy 4:7, "I have fought a good fight. I have finished the course. I have kept the faith." That says it all.

APPLICATION: As you pray today, ask God to help you to be a Christlike example to others. It will have an effect on others when you do so, and they will never forget the good you did for them. Look for someone today who you can affect for eternity.

WEEK 45—FRIDAY

Be a Lighthouse

SCRIPTURE READING: Matthew 5:11–16
THREE KEY WORDS: Light—Love—Life

I. Light

Before we were saved, we walked in darkness. We thought we were happy, life was fun while we were eating, drinking, and being merry. Then, one day, the Lord showed us the light of life, and when we accepted Christ as Lord and Savior, the brightness of real life—love, joy, peace, gentleness and kindness—came into our lives. We did not need to be afraid of the dark any longer. Now it is our job to take the light of Christ to others.

II. Love

One of the best ways to share our light of Christ is to be like Christ and love our neighbors as ourselves. We are to show them love by listening to them, helping them through prayer, and also helping them financially. Most of all, to be a true friend to them we should show them the love of Jesus, so they can have the light of salvation as well.

III. Life

Life can be *dark, dreary* and *difficult* for a lot of people. As disciples of Christ, we are to turn their darkness to light, their dreary outlook on life to love, and their difficult lives into abundant lives here and in heaven by sharing the light of the gospel. Let's try to do it today.

APPLICATION: Ask God in your prayer time today to give you a loving spirit and a heart full of light so that you can go share with someone else the true meaning of life by living for Christ. As a lighthouse stands out in the darkness of the sea, let's be a lighthouse in someone's dark life today.

WEEK 46—MONDAY
Stay Out of God's Way

SCRIPTURE READING: 1 Samuel 24
THREE KEY WORDS: Wait—Will—Work

I. Wait

As we read today's scriptures, the point is that God always has a better way to do things than we do. Our problem is that we don't want to wait for God's way. Just like children, we want it our way. Waiting is one of the hardest things to do. That is why God made patience a virtue. The Bible says, "Wait and be still and know I am God."

II. Will

God has a will for our lives in everything we do and in every decision we have to make—where we live, our vacations, our families, and our desires in life. We need to seek His will and way, because the path we follow with God can be a lot easier instead of us making a path of our own. We need to wait and seek God's will.

III. Work

The Bible is very clear that God's way and will is what works best for us. He knew all our days before we were ever born, and He has a wonderful way for us. Today, let's say, "Okay, God, I am waiting. Show me your will and let's work together." Let God be first. Get out of His way.

APPLICATION: As you pray today, ask God to show you specific areas of your life that are not surrendered to His will and way. Make a list of those things and then simply hand them back to Him and tell Him that you are going to wait for His will because that is what works.

WEEK 46—TUESDAY

Prayer Formula

SCRIPTURE READING: 1 Peter 3
THREE KEY WORDS: Honor—Help—Hinder

I. Honor

We hear and read many different ways to have a successful prayer life, but in today's scripture Peter tells us there are some important qualifications for God to hear our prayers. One of these is by honoring our wives. My wife and I have been married for forty-four years. She is absolutely beautiful on the inside and walks closest with the Lord of anyone I know. This is a quality that I should honor about her at all times.

II. Help

We are also to help our wives in many ways. Peter says they are the weaker vessels. My wife is the same size today that she was forty-four years ago—4'9" tall, and 94 pounds. She is one of the strongest women I know mentally, spiritually, and physically, but she is not as physically strong as I am. Therefore, I am to honor and help her as the weaker vessel. That doesn't mean being superior to her, but as a servant to help her.

III. Hinder

Peter says if we do those things that our prayers won't be hindered, but honored by Christ. Check your spirit about your relationship with your wife. Don't be a hindrance, but be helpful and honor your wife and God will answer your prayers.

APPLICATION: If you are not helping or honoring your wife, as you have personal time with the Lord, ask Him to forgive you of this sin and to help you to honor your wife. Then, go to your wife and ask her forgiveness as well, and make a commitment from this day forward to honor and help her.

WEEK 46—WEDNESDAY

The Church

SCRIPTURE READING: Matthew 16:13–20
THREE KEY WORDS: Change—Challenge—Church

I. **Change**
In today's world, everything is changing. In fact, change happens so fast we can't keep up with it. In business and family life, we constantly go through change. The fact is if we don't change in business, we can go down the tubes, and in family, we can face problems. Change can be good or bad depending on how we receive it.

II. **Challenge**
Frankly, it is a challenge for some of us to go through change. I have found it difficult for me with computer technology and even in my spiritual life. People say we need to change the method, not the message. Some of the methods—music, television and dress codes—are difficult for me, but God never changes. He is the same yesterday, today, and tomorrow.

III. **Church**
Jesus said the church will never change. The method, music, and ministers might change, but the one thing we can count on is that the body of Christ the gospel—will live forever. Praise God.

APPLICATION: Today, if you are facing the challenge of change in your life, whether at work, home, or at church, ask God to give you the patience you need to do so. Accept the fact that it is going to happen anyway, and adjust your attitude from a negative challenge to a positive outlook by accepting the change and moving forward with it.

WEEK 46—THURSDAY

Be Patient—God Is in Control

SCRIPTURE READING: 1 Samuel 20–28
THREE KEY WORDS: Waiting—Watching—Worshipping

I. Waiting

The hardest thing in life sometimes is simply waiting. I get so frustrated when I wait in traffic, or sometimes waiting on another person, or waiting for a decision to be made at work. Waiting can be frustrating or fruitful. In my car, I turn frustration into fruit by listening to a tape or message. In today's scripture, Hannah waited for years to have a child, and her waiting turned into a fruitful blessing with Samuel.

II. Watching

Sometimes God is asking us to watch for what He wants us to do. In waiting, He might be testing us or getting ready to show us His will for our future. My pastor says that while waiting on God, watch for confirming signs from God, through His Word, circumstances, and other people who come into our lives. While waiting, be watching.

III. Worshipping

Another thing we can do to turn frustration into fruit while waiting is to worship. Many times while stuck in traffic I will put in a great worship CD and have a spirit-filled meeting right there in my car. While waiting, think of something you can praise and worship God for, and then have a time of praise and worship right there, and your frustration will turn into contentment.

APPLICATION: If you are waiting for something in your life today, such as a decision at work, a report from your doctor, or what to do for your future, ask God to speak to you through His Word, or to give you a confirming sign. Be watchful while you are waiting, and when He makes it clear, take time to worship Him.

WEEK 46—FRIDAY
The Forbidden Things in Life

SCRIPTURE READING: Romans 7:7–13
THREE KEY WORDS: Flesh—Fruit—Feast

I. **Flesh**
In today's scripture, Paul talks about the flesh and how the flesh wants to test the forbidden. The speed limit is posted at 55 miles per hour, but we want to go 70. The Bible says not to look upon a woman with lust, but the flesh gets aroused when we see a beautiful woman. The law is not to test us, but to protect us and also guide us to live for God. God's grace helps us to keep the law.

II. **Fruit**
I think a good example of this is when Adam and Eve had everything a person could want in life. They lived in a beautiful garden, had a close walk with God, and the fruit of the spirit in their lives. They only had one law to live by—don't eat the fruit of the tree. But just like with us, Satan got them to let the flesh take over the fruit and they committed sin. Since then, that has been and will always be a daily battle.

III. **Feast**
Jesus says, however, come feast with me. Give your heart and soul to me and I will give you the abundant life here and a feast in heaven. When the flesh says *sin*, the savior says *surrender*, and the spirit says enjoy my fruit.

APPLICATION: As you pray today, ask God to help you overcome any fleshly desires that come your way. "Draw near to Him and He will draw near to you." When this happens, you will walk in the fruit of the Spirit and have a feast with Him all day long. What a blessing.

WEEK 47—MONDAY

Prayer

SCRIPTURE READING: Matthew 7:7–11
THREE KEY WORDS: Everyone—Effort—Effective

I. Everyone
As we read in today's scripture, prayer is for everyone. Jesus says everyone who asks, receives, and he who seeks, finds. There is one important qualification, however, and that is we must be a child of God or born again for our Father to hear our prayer. The Father is waiting to answer His children as lovingly and kindly as we answer our own children.

II. Effort
The second qualification for a meaningful prayer life is that it takes effort. We sometimes give a simple prayer at mealtime or bedtime, but if we want God to hear and respond, it takes effort. We must set aside a time with God, and make an appointment to just talk to Him and pour out our hearts and emotions to Him. It is not always easy, but it is worth it.

III. Effective
To emphasize effort, the Bible says "the effective fervent prayer of a righteous man availeth much." It has to be fervent to be effective. We do have the promise from the Father that if we make the effort, and come to Him asking, seeking, and knocking, we will be effective and get answers.

APPLICATION: All of us want an effective prayer life. As you start this new week, make a new effort to be effective by setting aside a special time and place to spend ten to twenty minutes praying to your Father. Also keep a prayer list, as it will let you see firsthand just how effective your effort has been as you see the answers come.

WEEK 47—TUESDAY
Life After Death

SCRIPTURE READING: John 11:25–44
THREE KEY WORDS: Reassurance—Resurrection—Reunited

I. Reassurance
In today's scripture, Jesus gives the reassurance that death is like waking up from a deep sleep. He says that if we believe in Him, we will never die. What reassurance to the Christian who might be facing death or has just lost a loved one. The reassurance that even though the body is dead, the spirit is very much alive.

II. Resurrection
We also have the reassurance that all of us will be resurrected some day, just like Jesus had the power to resurrect Lazarus from the grave. Some day Jesus will return. Graves will open, and we will be resurrected to be with Him forever in our beautiful mansion in heaven. What reassurance from the Father—that the resurrection will soon be here.

III. Reunited
We also have the reassurance that we will be reunited with our loved ones who have died before us—our grandparents, parents, brothers or sisters, family, and friends. What reassurance we have that death is not a dreadful thing but a delightful experience for the believer because of Jesus and His death, burial, and resurrection.

APPLICATION: As you pray today, thank God for the reassurance that some day you will be resurrected and reunited with Him in heaven. Also, make a commitment to tell others so they can enjoy this same reassurance. We must do it for ourselves, but more importantly, for others.

WEEK 47—WEDNESDAY

TV Guidance

SCRIPTURE READING: Ephesians 5:1–12
THREE KEY WORDS: Viewer—Value—Victory

I. Viewer

Each day when I finally sit down to relax, I often turn on the television. For the next two hours, I will exercise my thumb more than other parts of my body. That "exercise" is called channel-surfing and is done by millions of people daily. The question is, "Where do I pause while surfing? Do I feed my mind with something good or does something entice me to stray and look where I shouldn't?" In today's scripture, God makes it very clear to us where we should not pause—if it has sexual implications, foul language, greed, etc., we are to pass it by.

II. Value

Sometimes as I spend those two hours surfing, I ask myself, "What value am I getting from this that is going to make me better? Is this going to build me up or tear me down? Is this something that can add to my character? Will it help me or harm me?" As we surf the channels on TV, the viewers' guidelines should be, "What value am I getting from this, and would I watch this if Jesus were sitting next to me?" Remember, He is inside you.

III. Victory

Our guidelines are outlined in Ephesians 5 as what to watch. Also, we can get a victory over this by walking in the light. When we walk in the light of Christ, the viewer will only watch things of value, and have victory over the evil one.

APPLICATION: As a family, sit down and go through the *TV Guide* and determine what shows you will watch and what is not acceptable. Also determine the amount of time you will spend watching television. If you are alone, be sure and have an accountability partner you report to concerning the shows you watch. This will help you attain victory.

WEEK 47—THURSDAY

The Ministry of Encouragement

SCRIPTURE READING: 1 Thessalonians Chapter 1
THREE KEY WORDS: Condemn—Correct—Counsel

I. Condemn

My good friend Zig Ziglar always said that we live in a cat-kicking world. In other words, we are always looking for the bad in people and not the good. We focus on the negative and not the positive. When one of our kids does something wrong, we say you always do that; when in reality, it doesn't happen much at all. The world is full of hurting people because of the condemnation they face daily from others.

II. Correct

We need to correct our thinking and our attitude toward others. There are two types of people in this world—people who are problem-oriented and people who are solution-oriented. We need to become solution-oriented mentors by telling people the good they do and the good qualities they have, and it will start when we correct our thoughts and focus on the good.

III. Counsel

The ministry of encouragement is a must. Millions of people go to bed every night who are starving for food, but many more millions go to bed every night starving for recognition and appreciation. Today, let's commit to not condemn, but to correct our thinking and counsel people we come into contact with daily. It will not only help them, but will be a tremendous blessing to you as well.

APPLICATION: As you come into contact with people today, ask yourself, "How can I encourage this person?" Then say something positive and pleasant to them to lift their spirits. They will be glad you did and so will you.

WEEK 47—FRIDAY

Our Job—God's Job

SCRIPTURE READING: John 3:1–17
THREE KEY WORDS: Frustration—Faithful—Fruitful

I. Frustration
Many times as Christians we meet or know a number of people who are not believers. We want so badly for them to know salvation so they can spend eternity in heaven. We try everything: Bible tracts, special events at church, and witnessing to them one on one. As a result, we become frustrated, and the more frustrated we become, the harder it is for them and us. It might even cause us family problems or cost us a friendship.

II. Faithful
The main job we have each day is to be a witness for our Lord. Our life and the way we live it is the best witness of all. However, God says that our main job is to plant the seed of His Word every day and to be faithful in doing so. Just like the farmer plants seeds to get a harvest, we must plant seeds to see people come to Christ. Therefore, our job is to plant and pray.

III. Fruitful
If we do our job, and plant the seeds, God will do His job to bring in the harvest. As you read today's scripture, you can almost feel the frustration of Jesus as He talks to a prominent religious leader who could not understand this simple process. Man produces human life, but the Holy Spirit gives life from Heaven. It is our job to plant and pray, it is God's job to bring in the harvest through his Holy Spirit.

APPLICATION: As we go into the marketplace today, let's plant a lot of seeds of the gospel. As I said earlier, this can be through our living by an example, helping someone in need, talking with them or giving them a tract. Then pray that the Holy Spirit will bring the harvest.

WEEK 48—MONDAY

The Three L's of Christian Character

SCRIPTURE READING: Luke 2:41–52
THREE KEY WORDS: Likeable—Loveable—Learnable

I. Likeable
One of the things we must work on daily as Christians is to be likable. We must strive to like others and, as well, get them to like us. We can't witness to someone if they don't like us. Sometimes, because of our dogmatic stance, we turn people off and they will ignore us or try to avoid us. It is very important to be likable.

II. Loveable
There is a difference between likeable and loveable. In loving others, we have the heart of Jesus that we will do anything we need to do to bring them into the kingdom. Also, we can love the unlikable by being a friend to them, meeting a need they might have, and telling them about the love of Jesus and how He died for them. When we love the unlikable with unconditional love, we can change them into likeable and loveable people.

III. Learnable
We must continue daily to learn from God's Word and also to learn from the people who cross our path daily. Remember, school is always in session for the Christian.

APPLICATION: As you pray today, ask God for your spirit to be likeable and loveable. As you come into contact with people, radiate the character of Christ that says: no matter what happens, I like you and love you unconditionally. This character will draw people to you as it drew people to Christ.

WEEK 48—TUESDAY

Jesus Is Calling

SCRIPTURE READING: John 10:1–11
THREE KEY WORDS: Help—Heed—Hear

I. Help
As we go about our work and duties, there are times when we need help. We might be frustrated at work, have financial pressures, don't feel well, and we feel like screaming "Help! I can't go it alone anymore. I need someone's help." The best help is just a quick prayer away.

II. Heed
Jesus said in today's scripture that when I need help, I am to heed His voice. I am the sheep and He is the shepherd. He calls me by name and says heed my voice. Financial problems—I will supply your need; health, by my stripes you are healed; loneliness, I will never leave you nor forsake you. Jesus is calling. Heed His call today and follow him.

III. Hear
One other thing we need to do is to quietly listen for Jesus' voice so we can hear Him. In prayer, listen for that still small voice. When reading the Bible, listen to what He is saying through His Word. "Be still and know I am God." Sometimes we listen, but we don't hear. Our minds are somewhere else. When talking to God, praying, or listening to God through the Word, don't just listen, but hear the voice of God our good shepherd.

APPLICATION: If you feel as though you are in a helpless situation today, cry out to God and tell Him you need Him more than ever. Open up to Him all the way. Be totally sincere. Let go of the situation and surrender it to Him. Then sit back and listen for the still small voice that will bring you peace.

WEEK 48—WEDNESDAY

Count Your Blessings

SCRIPTURE READING: Peter 1:1–9
THREE KEY WORDS: Remember—Rejoice—Resurrection

I. Remember

Whenever we seem to be singing the blues, one of the things we need to do is to remember where we were before we became a Christian. The Gaithers have a song that says, "When I think of where he brought me from to where I am today, that's the reason why I love Him so." When I look back and think where I was before giving my life to Christ, I should never complain, because even when I have a tough day now, it is nothing like before.

II. Rejoice

When we stop and remember the above, we should rejoice. Today's scripture talks about rejoicing. I know it is hard to live by the scripture, and rejoice. We don't always feel like it, but if we *remember* that *receiving* Christ is reason enough to *rejoice* daily. Just focus on that one thing alone and we will rejoice.

III. Resurrection

Remember and then rejoice. Why? Because when we received Jesus, He made us a reservation in heaven. My Father's house has many rooms, and I have a special one just for you. As we meditate on that, we should rejoice and shout: "hallelujah, oh what a savior!"

APPLICATION: If you feel down and out today, take time in your prayer to simply stop and remember where you were before receiving Christ as savior. Remember how you felt, how you changed, and all the wonderful things He has done for you. Then have a special time of rejoicing.

WEEK 48—THURSDAY
Overcoming Fear

SCRIPTURE READING: John 6:16–21
THREE KEY WORDS: Fear—Failure—Freedom

I. Fear
Throughout my life, I have fought fear. As a young boy growing up, my mom always said that when I did something wrong, God was going to punish me. So, for many years, I was trapped in fear. Everybody faces fear of some kind—death, finances, loss of job, etc., but fear is from the devil. My friend Zig Ziglar says that F.E.A.R. is "False Evidence Appearing Real." Satan gives us false evidence that appears real, but God defeats Satan and He says we need not fear.

II. Failure
Sometimes fear causes us to fail. We get so tired and battle-weary, that we finally give into that fear and give up, but God says that He understands, and He will restore. Again quoting my friend Zig, "Failure is an event, not a person." The fact is that in life we will fail, but we can use our failures as learning experiences to succeed. It is okay to fail.

III. Freedom
There is freedom through Jesus Christ. "Come to me all who are heavy-laden, and I will give you rest." We need to cast all our fears on Christ because He said, "I can do all things through Christ Jesus, including defeating fear." Give Him your fear today and get a victory over fear.

APPLICATION: To overcome fear, we must face it head on. First, we must confess the fear to the Lord and ask Him for the strength to overcome that fear. He has promised to do so. If we have failed, it doesn't mean we are a failure. Ask Christ to forgive you and start again, fresh and new. Then you will feel the freedom of the Holy Spirit in your life.

WEEK 48—FRIDAY

No Favorites with God

SCRIPTURE READING: James 2
THREE KEY WORDS: People—Partial—Pure

I. People
In our everyday world, we run into all different types of people: rich and poor, overweight and slim, introverts and extroverts, and all different races. But God is very clear in today's scripture that in His eyes we are all the same. He also instructs us to treat all people the same.

II. Partial
Jesus was not partial to anyone. He ministered to the rich, the lepers, the poor, and crossed all racial barriers because He loved everyone. We are the ones who make it difficult. We see a famous person and think he or she is great, we see the homeless and we walk right on by, but God says we commit sin when we do that. If God has no favorites on earth, we shouldn't either. When we come into contact with people, we should just ask God, Father, how can I help this person today?

III. Pure
Jesus paid a high price on the cross and died for each of us. God so loved the world, everyone from everywhere, that Jesus paid the price on Calvary so we could all have the opportunity to enjoy the wonderful rewards in heaven. Reach out to everyone today.

APPLICATION: The scripture clearly commands us to be a respecter of people. Remember the eyes of Jesus look at everyone the same. Ask Him to give you those same eyes so we can love and meet the needs of everyone. That's what Jesus would do.

WEEK 49—MONDAY

Lifting People Higher

SCRIPTURE READING: Acts 28:11–16
THREE KEY WORDS: Heavy—Heart—Higher

I. **Heavy**
As people go through life each day, many of them carry very heavy loads. They have burdens of financial troubles, health problems, family relationships and loneliness. Sometimes I get so heavy with loneliness I ask myself, How can I take another step? Our burdens get so heavy on our shoulders and we might lose sight of who can help us carry the load.

II. **Heart**
When your heart is troubled and the load is heavy, look to the cross. Think of the load that Jesus carried to Calvary with the weight of all our sins on His shoulders. It will help us realize that when our load is heavy, it can be light because Jesus said to cast all of our cares and burdens on Him for His yoke is light. We can surrender our heavy hearts to Jesus and He will lift us up.

III. **Higher**
As the song says, "I am stepping on the upward way, new height I'm gaining every day." Lord, lead me on to higher ground. Our job as Christians is to find people who are carrying a heavy load, encourage them, pray with them, love them, and together both of us can go higher and higher with Jesus.

APPLICATION: If you feel a burden so heavy that you can't bear it, look to the cross of Jesus. Remember the heavy load of His own cross as He went up Golgotha. Remember the weight of our sin on His shoulders and then remember He did it for you to lighten your load. I promise you it will do so.

WEEK 49—TUESDAY
Our Hiding Place

SCRIPTURE READING: Psalm 57
THREE KEY WORDS: Pursuit—Plead—Presence

I. Pursuit
It seems there are times in our lives that Satan is constantly pursuing us. It could be through sickness, financial problems, family relationships, temptations, etc. The Bible says that Satan is like a roaring lion seeking whom He may devour. In other words, Satan is on a *prowl*, *pursuing* us through *problems*, waiting for us to weaken so he can destroy us. It is a fact as well that the more you pursue God, the more Satan will pursue you.

II. Plead
When the *pain* of Satan's *pursuit* gets too hard for us to bear, the best thing we can do is *plead* with God through *prayer*. Tell God how painful it is, how much pressure you are under. The Bible says resist the devil and he will flee from you. Draw nigh unto God and He will draw nigh unto you. You might think that it is so hard. If so, remember God's promise—greater is He who is in you than he that is in the world. God will make a way for you to escape.

III. Presence
When you pray, ask God for His presence to be so real to you during this time. We must remember that God is our refuge, a hiding place in our time of *pain*, *problems* and *pressure*. As the song says, in the presence of Jehovah, troubles vanish. That doesn't mean they will go away, but it promises that His presence is with us to triumph over the pursuit of Satan.

APPLICATION: As you pray today, put on your spiritual clothing—the helmet of salvation, the shield of faith, the belt of truth, and the shoes of the gospel. If Satan pursues you today, plead with God for help and claim victory through the power of the Holy Spirit because of the victory we have through Christ Jesus.

WEEK 49—WEDNESDAY

How to Respond to Criticism

SCRIPTURE READING: Amos 7
THREE KEY WORDS: Unpleasant—Unpopular—Uplifting

I. **Unpleasant**
   When we receive criticism for what we say or do, it can be very unpleasant; in fact, it can be very hurtful and painful. Constructive criticism can be good, but it is still sometimes unpleasant. No one likes to be lied to, gossiped about, or just plain criticized. Much will depend on how we handle the criticism about us. God says very clearly that we should go right to the source and get the matter cleared immediately.

II. **Unpopular**
   Criticism can also make us unpopular, whether we are the giver or receiver. If we are the giver of criticism, some people won't appreciate us for criticizing someone else. If we are the receiver of the criticism, we will do one of two things when we hear it: respond or react. Responding is positive, as we let it roll off our backs and continue on. We will be respected for doing so. If we react and act negatively about the criticism, we can retaliate and become unpopular.

III. **Uplifting**
   If we respond in a positive way, we could use the criticism to uplift others. There is a saying that says praise in public, criticize in private. If you follow this simple formula, you can uplift others by responding in a positive and uplifting way when receiving criticism. Keep a good attitude when criticized.

APPLICATION: If someone criticizes you today, remember to respond and not react. Let it help you instead of hinder you. If you need to give constructive criticism to someone, remember to do it privately not publicly. Don't be unpleasant, instead be uplifting.

WEEK 49—THURSDAY

When Life Is a Bore

SCRIPTURE READING: Ecclesiastes 1
THREE KEY WORDS: Fresh—Faithful—Fruitful

I. Fresh

Day after day, life can become *dreary, depressing* or *delightful*. I heard someone say life is getting up, going to work, coming home, watching TV, having dinner, going to bed, and repeating the same process over and over again. If that is the way we see life, we will be *depressed* and *discouraged*. We must look at each day as a fresh start, to enjoy what God has provided for us that day and remember that at the end of that day, we are one step closer to our home in Heaven.

II. Faithful

Each day we must be faithful by surrendering our will to God's. God will bring little fresh things into our day that will be exciting to us, if we just exercise our faith that God's daily plan is better than our daily plan. Be faithful to God's purpose for our lives. It will give you a fresh start every day.

III. Fruitful

If we exercise our faith each day, our work will be fruitful. God will answer our prayers, bring someone into our lives we can witness to, and give us an opportunity to meet someone's needs. It is a joy when we can look at each day and ask God, "What do you have for me today?" God will bring fresh opportunities to us if we do so.

APPLICATION: As you pray today, remember that there is nothing you can do about yesterday, and we don't even know if there will be a tomorrow. Therefore, do your best to have a great time all day long and enjoy your day to the fullest.

WEEK 49—FRIDAY
Spiritual Fitness

SCRIPTURE READING: Psalm 119:97–110
THREE KEY WORDS: Fitness—Fatness—Fruitfulness

I. Fitness

I recently read an article that said we lose 60 percent of our muscle mass during our 60s. Therefore, when I turned 60, I made a commitment to a stretching and exercise program every morning. In the morning I do 20 minutes of stretching, and in the evening 20 minutes of exercise. We need to do the same in our spiritual life as well. The longer we are Christians, we can approach our spiritual life casually or conditioned. This book came as a result of every morning studying God's Word and praying faithfully from 6:00 A.M. to 7:00 A.M. It took 18 months of work, but it made me fit for the day.

II. Fatness

Just as we can get fat from neglecting diet and exercise, we can also get fat from not being spiritually fit. We may compromise our beliefs, our value system changes, or God's Word means nothing to us. Before long we become complacent Christians and not committed Christians, all because we don't exercise spiritually.

III. Fruitful

In physical exercise we will enjoy the fruits of our efforts. We lose weight, we breathe better, our endurance and stamina increase, and we feel a sense of accomplishment. The same is true when we exercise in prayer and daily Bible reading. We will love God more. We will be faithful and fruitful for Him. It is not easy, but will pay great dividends.

APPLICATION: Today, make a total commitment to physical and spiritual fitness. If you are not on an exercise program physically, start immediately. Also, make a spiritual commitment to fitness by starting each day with a minimum of twenty minutes of prayer and Bible study. It will increase your strength for winning spiritual battles.

WEEK 50—MONDAY

Insensitive to Sin

SCRIPTURE READING: Romans 8:1–26
THREE KEY WORDS: Recognize—Restore—Repent

I. Recognize
We must recognize that sin is everywhere. Immodesty has become so popular that it is affecting and infecting the Christian. Billboards, music videos, television, and the internet can all be temptations. If we are not careful, we will let little sins creep in and pretty soon, we will become insensitive to what we used to take a strong stand for. If we don't take action now, we could be asking for trouble later. We must take a stand against sin.

II. Restore
We need to ask God to restore our strong conviction against sin. We need to return to our first love in our lives, and that is our love for Christ and the Holy Spirit. We must not lose our first love. Remember how it was when you first were saved—how excited you were and how you stood for what was right? Ask God to restore that same excitement back into your spirit.

III. Repent
I know that some of us have stumbled and fallen. We might be hooked on music videos, or even have committed an act of infidelity with the opposite sex, but it is never too late. God will recognize our sincerity, restore our joy, if only we will repent and give our lives to Him. It is never too late.

APPLICATION: As you pray today, ask God to restore the excitement you once had for Him and living for Him by taking a stand for what is right. Also, recognize some areas in your life where you are weak, and ask God to help you to overcome those weaknesses. Return to your first love and be fruitful for Him.

WEEK 50—TUESDAY

Have a Heart for Others

SCRIPTURE READING: Romans 9:1–10
THREE KEY WORDS: Sincerity—Sacrifice—Solution

I. Sincerity

One of the things that Paul points out in this scripture is the fact that we are to have a sincere burden and heart to reach others for Christ. He had a longing for his Jewish friends to come to Christ. We should have the same longing for our friends and family. Paul grieved and wept for this cause. His ministry was one of sincere love and concern for their souls.

II. Sacrifice

Paul said that if he could, he would be willing to sacrifice his own eternal salvation for them to come to Christ. In other words, he would sacrifice heaven and go to hell if they would give their lives to Jesus. That is real sincerity in caring for others. Jesus did that for us when He sacrificed His life on the cross for you and me. He literally came from heaven to earth and then went down into hell for us, but, praise the Lord, He was resurrected from hell and is in heaven. He made that sacrifice so we could trade hell for heaven.

III. Solution

It is through this sincere burden and sacrifice that we now have our salvation. Paul is saying, however, that we should not be satisfied with just that solution. We can't become complacent. People are going to hell every day. We must be sincere and sacrifice our time and dollars to bring salvation to as many people as possible.

APPLICATION: Today, ask God for a sincere heart and burden to reach the unsaved for Christ. It is a fact that people go to hell every day. The solution for us is to make whatever sacrifice we need to make to reach the lost. Let's make that commitment today.

WEEK 50—WEDNESDAY

Observing People

SCRIPTURE READING: Romans 12:1–8
THREE KEY WORDS: Observation—Ordinary—Other

I. Observation
Sometimes we get so busy in the game of life that we just take everything for granted. We don't see what is going on around us, let alone observe the needs of other people around us. Sometimes we just need to take time and ask ourselves, How do people observe me and how do I observe other people? Do they see me as being so busy that I don't have time for them, or do they see me as someone who really cares about people? Observations from others tell a lot about our Christlike character.

II. Ordinary
The Bible says that God uses ordinary people, such as the common person who gets up, goes to the factory or office every day, puts in a hard day's work, then goes home and spends time with family, or takes time to go to church, or helps a person in need. Jesus led an ordinary life here on earth when He could have had a life of fame as a King. Jesus worked with ordinary people like us so we need to be available for His use.

III. Other
Jesus always put others before Himself and we should as well. I was given a plaque that hangs on my wall that says, "Others, Lord, others. Let this my motto be, that I might live for others and more like Jesus be." That is our mission as Christians.

APPLICATION: As you come into contact with people today, ask yourself this question—how do these people observe me or see me? Am I too busy or am I available if they need me? Observe them as well and see if they have a need that you can meet. If so, be a person like Jesus was.

WEEK 50—THURSDAY

True Worship

SCRIPTURE READING: Psalm 47
THREE KEY WORDS: Thankfulness—Tenderness—Truthfulness

I. Thankfulness

When we worship God in our quiet time, and in our praise and worship at church, we should give our best. Many times our thoughts are somewhere else and our hearts are not really in it. When we pray in the morning, our minds are thinking about all we have to do that day. When we sing and praise God at church, our thoughts might be, "I don't like this kind of music, or the words. Why don't they sing the old hymns like they used to?" Be thankful to God and for what He has done for you. Then praise Him with all your heart.

II. Tenderness

When we offer praise and worship to God, our hearts should be tender toward Him. Just like we show tenderness when we praise our children, we should show tenderness when we praise our Father. If our hearts are true to Him, we sometimes will weep during our praise and worship, because we will feel the tenderness of Jesus speaking to our hearts. Just turn your heart to Him.

III. Truthfulness

Sometimes we are not truthful in our praise and worship. In other words, we are just moving our lips or standing and looking at others. God wants truthfulness in everything. If we can't truthfully give it our all, it is better not to do anything at all. As Jesus said, I want you, hot or cold, not lukewarm or I will spew you out of my mouth. Be *thoughtful,* be *tender,* and be *truthful* in your praise and worship to God.

APPLICATION: As you praise God today, whether in church or in your private time, ask God to give you a tender heart. Be thankful for what He has done for you. Block everything out of your heart and mind. Then, lift your voice to Him in song and prayer and have a wonderful time of praise and worship for which you will be thankful.

WEEK 50—FRIDAY
The Pressure Cooker

SCRIPTURE READING: 1 King 12:6–16
THREE KEY WORDS: Pressure—Power—Path

I. Pressure
In today's busy world, we live in a pressure cooker. We get up early, maybe have our devotion, take a quick shower, run out the door with a cup of coffee in our hand, get angry as we sit in traffic, finally get to work where there are meetings, problems, or a phone in both ears. Then we fight our way back home to a night of a relaxation with the remote and channel surf. Is that what life is all about? We let our peers at work or our pride dictate how much pressure we get under each day. Are we trying to keep up with the Joneses or Christ?

II. Power
We feel that by all we do daily, it will bring us some great power. It might be the power of money or prestige, big cars and having country club memberships, or the best for our kids. It can also be the power of telling people what to do or popularity in the secular world. All of this power is of the flesh and results in pressure that wears us out. The real power comes only from the Holy Spirit and His love.

III. Path
God wants us to take a different path. He says *power, prestige, pride,* and *position* are not important, but *people* are. He says that our relationships with people, whether family or friends, is what really counts. If you want to avoid the pressure cooker, He says, "Trust in me with all your heart, and lean not unto your own understanding. In all your ways, acknowledge Him and He will direct your path." He is the answer.

APPLICATION: If you feel like the lid is ready to blow because of being in the pressure cooker, exchange your personal power of the flesh for the pure power of the Holy Spirit. Ask Him to fill you up. Release the power in every area of your life and you will go from the *cooker* to the *comforter,* and life will be *calm* for you. Do so today.

WEEK 51—MONDAY
The Shepherds

SCRIPTURE READING: Luke 2
THREE KEY PHRASES: Shepherds—Savior—Security

I. Shepherds

Why would God choose shepherds to speak to? They were considered heathens like prostitutes and habitual sinners. They were outcasts. Many of us were the same before God spoke to us. We were just plain sinners. But, like the shepherds, we were longing for something else in our lives. Like the shepherds, we found it.

II. Savior

God sent us the Savior in Jesus so we could satisfy that longing in our soul. Just like the shepherds, one day the Word of God shone brightly and we knew God was speaking to us through the Holy Spirit. We met the Savior, just like the shepherds, and we saw Him through a changed life—our longing satisfied. I am so thankful.

III. Security

Because the Savior was born, died on the cross, and rose again, I can now have serenity and peace in my life. I can surrender all of my burdens to Him to ease the load, but most of all, I have the serenity and peace that some day I will be in heaven with Him. Oh, what a Savior.

APPLICATION: "The Lord is my shepherd, I shall not want." If this is true in your life, then let the Shepherd lead you as He does His flock. Look to the Savior and feel the security of knowing that you are in His will. The shepherd never fails us.

WEEK 51—TUESDAY

Getting Ready For Christmas

SCRIPTURE READING: Luke 2
THREE KEY WORDS: Preparation—Priority—Place

I Preparation
This time of year we hear a lot about preparing for Christmas—shopping, wrapping, writing Christmas cards, etc., but the most important preparation of all is preparing ourselves. We get so busy that we forget to prepare ourselves spiritually to enjoy the true meaning of Christmas. Like John the Baptist said, "We must prepare the way for the coming of the Messiah."

II. Priority
As we begin to celebrate Jesus coming to earth, we need to prepare ourselves by having a pure heart. John said to repent, confess our sins, clean our hearts, and be as pure as possible. Surrender it to God and celebrate Christmas in its true meaning.

III. Place
As we prepare for Christmas, Christ doesn't want second place in our hearts; He wants first place in our hearts. This is the best gift we can give Him and the best way to prepare for a great Christmas. We can never forget that of all the gifts we have received, our salvation and eternal life is the greatest gift of all. Make that the focus this Christmas.

APPLICATION: Before we get caught up in the busyness of Christmas—parties, presents and people, let's first prepare spiritually by making Christ the priority of the Christmas season. As the saying goes: "He is the reason for the season."

WEEK 51—WEDNESDAY

Effective Prayers

SCRIPTURE READING: John 3:21–24
THREE KEY PHRASES: Our Conscience—Our Condition—Our Confidence

I. Our Conscience

To have an effective prayer life, our conscience must be clean. We must not have any guilt about our sins, we must not have any doubts about our faith and our Christian walk. Our conscience must be crystal clear that everything is right with God.

II. Our Condition

Matthew 7:7-8 says that we will receive from God what we ask of Him, but there are conditions. First, in today's scripture, we must obey God and do what pleases Him. That means believing totally in Jesus and also loving others. This also produces a clear conscience. We must be obedient.

III. Our Confidence

In today's scripture, it says that if we follow the conditions and have a clear conscience, we can come to God with perfect assurance and trust, and get whatever we ask for because we are obeying Him and doing what pleases Him. To be effective, have a clear conscience—obey God's conditions, and be confident in His answer.

APPLICATION: Remember, in the scriptures it says, "the effectual, fervent prayer of a righteous man availeth much." Today, clear your conscience with confession. Meet God's condition of total love and obedience, and then be confident that He will hear and answer.

WEEK 51—THURSDAY

Yes or No

SCRIPTURE READING: John 5:24–30
THREE KEY PHRASES: Yearn for Christ—Yes to Christ—Yield to Christ

I. **Yearn For Christ**
As the scripture says, today, many of us yearn for Christ. We seek in the scriptures for peace, joy, guidance, direction, and solutions, but solution doesn't come by just yearning for Christ. He wants more.

II. **Yes To Christ**
In order to have a relationship with Christ, the Son of God, we must say yes to Him. We must accept Him as our personal Lord and Savior so we can build a personal relationship with Him. We must say yes, that He died for our sins and rose again, and ask for forgiveness. That is the real thing.

III. **Yield To Christ**
Now that we say yes to Christ, we must yield every part of our lives to Him. We must trust Him completely with our lives, give ourselves to the church and serve Him daily. We must not only know the facts, we also need to know the Savior. Yield today.

APPLICATION: If you are feeling a yearning to know Christ better, simply say yes to Him whether for salvation or service. Then, yield everything you have to Him so you can serve Him with mind, body and spirit. This will produce the most purposeful life possible and yield great benefits.

WEEK 51—FRIDAY

Life and Death Matters

SCRIPTURE READING: Romans 8:12–18
THREE KEY PHRASES: The Lie—The Lion—The Lord

I. The Lie
Satan is the biggest liar on earth. He makes everything in the world look good to us so we will yield to the flesh. It is a lie.

II. The Lion
In the jungle, animals must survive by killing their prey. Nature is violent. Something must die in the jungle so something else can live. The same is true spiritually. Satan roars like a lion to see who he can devour. In the jungle of our hearts, interests of the flesh must succumb to interests of the spirit. Something must die so something else can live.

III. The Lord
We need the Lord's help to die daily to the flesh. It is a constant battle. As I go into the jungle every day, I must say, Lord, I yield my spirit and flesh today. Help me to survive in the jungle—help me walk in the spirit today I pray, and not be pray to Satan.

APPLICATION: Face it—today we all go into some level of personal jungle. We need to be ready for the battle. Remember that Satan is a liar and the Savior is truth. Surrender to the Savior, not Satan, and you will succeed in your battle. Enjoy the victory along the way.

WEEK 52—MONDAY

God's Work

SCRIPTURE READING: Luke 19:41–48
THREE KEY PHRASES: God's Pursuit—God's Persistence—God's Promises

I. God's Pursuit

From the beginning of time, God has pursued His people. The Bible is full of stories about how God pursued His chosen people. God also pursues us in our lives. He makes us aware of our need for Christ and eternal life. He pursues us every day to live for Him and to surrender everything we have and everything we are, so He can use us.

II. God's Persistence

God loves us so much that He is persistent in never giving up on us. Just like we were persistent in showing love and compassion to our spouses when we first met, so God is persistent with us to build a love relationship with Him as well. In His pursuit and persistence, He finally gave it all when He sent Jesus into the world to pay the ultimate price of love, by laying down His life for us, so that we could have an intimate love relationship with Father, Son, and Holy Spirit. Oh, what love.

III. God's Promises

If we accept Jesus as our Lord and Savior, than we are to love Him more than anything in the world. We now should be persistent in our pursuit of knowing God in a personal way. At the same time, we should be persistent in our pursuit to tell others about this wonderful love through the gospel. That's our goal each day.

APPLICATION: As God pursued us so we need to pursue others. We need to be persistent daily. In doing so, we also must remember His promise that His Word will never return void. It is a promise that if we persist in pursuing others that we will reach them. Let's do it daily.

WEEK 52—TUESDAY

Foot Washing

SCRIPTURE READING: John 13:1–20
THREE KEY WORDS: Servant—Savior—Saint

I. Servant

The practice of foot washing was part of the culture in Jesus' day. It was the lowliest job in a household. When guests came into the home, that person had to stoop and wash the feet of the people who had just come off of dirty and sandy streets. In today's scripture, we see the Savior become the servant because of His love for His disciples. Could we do the same for our friends?

II. Savior

In this scripture, the creator of the universe now becomes the compassionate, caring servant. It is hard for us to imagine that Christ could love so much that He told Peter that He must do it so Peter could be His partner. Jesus not only washed feet, but layed down His life on the cross and suffered the worse possible death, so I could be His brother. What love that is for us.

III. Saint

Because of that love for me and you, we can now become saints and spend eternity in heaven with our Savior forever. Jesus said, "In foot washing I have given you an example to follow." We must not forget to serve. Daily we need to follow the example of Jesus.

APPLICATION: As you spend time with God today, ask Him for a servant's spirit. Thank Him that because of His servant spirit we are now saints for His glory. To be saintly like Christ, we must be a servant by living the example he set. Have a servant's spirit today.

WEEK 52—WEDNESDAY

Come Alive

SCRIPTURE READING: Revelation 3:1–6
THREE KEY PHRASES: The Flame—The Fire—The Finish

I. The Flame
When we were first saved, God put a flame in our hearts. We were a new creature. Old things had passed away, all things became new. We were changed inside and out. We had new hearts, a new reason for living, we were different as new babes in Christ. We let the new spark of flame lead us into new knowledge of our faith.

II. The Fire
As we grew in our faith, our flame became a living fire. We love going to church, serving and praising the Lord, having fellowship with our Christian brothers and sisters. We can't wait for Sunday or Wednesday for the church to open so we can attend services. We also have a huge flame to tell others about Jesus—what He did for us and the new abundant life He gave us. Most of all, we have a fire to tell others about Christ and keep them from the fire of hell. That was a real motivator for us.

III. The Finish
As we get older in life and our faith, we become content and the flame gets low. It is no longer a fire. We don't witness like we should. We have become complacent. In today's scripture, God tells us to wake up, to stir the embers to a burning flame again and return to what we were when we were first saved. Lord, help me to have that fire for you once again.

APPLICATION: If the embers are low and the spark is gone, ask God to get you stirred up so you can be a burning fire. Remember your commitment to reaching others for Christ. I challenge you to make a list of five people you know and then go and witness to them. I promise you that if one accepts Christ, the embers will become a flaming fire once again for you and Christ.

WEEK 52—THURSDAY

The Mind

SCRIPTURE READING: Philippians 4:1–10
THREE KEY PHRASES: Our Minds—Our Mission—Our Master

I. Our Minds

The mind is the gateway to the heart. We are what we are and where we are because of what goes into our minds. We change what we are and where we are by changing what goes into our minds. We are faced with negative thoughts and actions daily. We must try to rearrange these things in our minds to be positive. It is like a computer and will act out what it is programmed to do. That is why Paul gave us instructions on what to put into our minds.

II. Our Mission

Our mission in life is to reach others for Christ, but we also have the mission of taking God's Word and putting it into action. We just don't read it, or study it, and not apply it. It is our instructions on how to live life to the fullest, so we should make it a daily mission.

III. Our Master

Our master is God Himself. We need to realize that He is in control of our lives every day. That is why Paul says, "Don't worry about anything, but in everything with prayer and supplication, turn your worries into prayer." Peace comes from knowing that God is in control. We need to let God guard us against worries. Happiness is a choice, and we find happiness in knowing God, and that He has nothing but the best in store for us. Give it all over to Him today.

APPLICATION: As you read the scripture and devotion today, ask God how you can put this into action. Say, Master, I have a mission, and that is to be positive, and also to be a good example to others. Help me to do so. Prepare the mind, prepare the heart, and go complete your mission of ministry.

WEEK 52—FRIDAY

The End

SCRIPTURE READING: 1 Peter 2:18–25
THREE KEY PHRASES: The Enemy—The Example—The Eternal

I. The Enemy

As we struggle through each day, week, month, and year, we are going to experience attacks from the enemy, Satan. In today's scripture, God gives us the example of what we sometimes face from our bosses or people in authority. Even if they are tough, cruel, unfair, we are to do what they ask. Sometimes Satan will allow those attacks to test our faith, and that is when we need to be strong.

II. The Example

In today's scripture it says that when this happens we are to praise the Lord if we are punished for doing right. It also says that Jesus is an example through the suffering He endured for us. He never sinned, never told a lie, never answered back when insulted, and when He was treated badly, even by the enemy, He never threatened or tried to get even. He simply turned it over to God to handle fairly. He is our example.

III. The Eternal

As we come to this final mini-message, my challenge to all of us is to realize that we will always fight the enemy, but because of the example of Christ and what He did on the cross for us, we have victory over the enemy. To make it here on earth each day, we must focus on our eternal home in heaven, where there will be no more attacks, unfair treatment, sickness or sorrow. We will have only *peace, praise,* and *pleasure* with our Savior, family and friends, for all eternity. What a message to end this book with.

APPLICATION: If you feel today that you are being attacked or treated unfairly, at work, home, or by friends, follow the example of Jesus and let God have control. Next, focus on the eternal and realize that some day it will be worth it all when we see Jesus. The only thing that counts is *faith, family,* and *friendships* for all eternity.

Dave Curry would like to invite you to order a copy of *Mini-Messages for Monday through Friday* for yourself or a friend. Please photocopy the order form, fill in the blanks (please print), and mail the order form to Dave along with a check or money order. If you would like to order a quantity of the book for your church or organization, please contact Dave at 303-697-4690 or by e-mail at **propres8@aol.com**.

PLEASE SHIP ONE COPY OF
Mini-Messages for Monday through Friday to:

NAME _____

ADDRESS _____

CITY, STATE, ZIP _____

PHONE NUMBER _____

Please send a check or money order for $19.00 (that includes shipping and handling) to:

           Dave Curry
           15703 West Wedge Way
           Morrison, CO 80465
      Please allow three weeks for delivery.

You can also contact Dave at the same number or e-mail to have him speak for your church, business, or organization.